The Lemonade Stand Millionaire

The Lemonade Stand Millionaire

A **Parents' Guide** to Encouraging
the Entrepreneurial Spirit in Your Kids

Gail Haynes

NEW YORK

The Lemonade Stand Millionaire
A Parents' Guide to Encouraging the Entrepreneurial Spirit in Your Kids

ISBN 978-1-61448-388-5 paperback
ISBN 978-1-61448-389-2 eBook
Library of Congress Control Number: 2012951720

Morgan James Publishing
The Entrepreneurial Publisher
5 Penn Plaza, 23rd Floor,
New York City, New York 10001
(212) 655-5470 office • (516) 908-4496 fax
www.MorganJamesPublishing.com

Illustrations by:
Adonis Howard
www.adonishoward.com

Cover Design by:
Brenda Haun
BHaundesigns@gmail.com

Interior Design by:
Bonnie Bushman
bonnie@caboodlegraphics.com

In an effort to support local communities, raise awareness and funds, Morgan James Publishing donates a percentage of all book sales for the life of each book to Habitat for Humanity Peninsula and Greater Williamsburg.

Get involved today, visit
www.MorganJamesBuilds.com.

Habitat
for Humanity®
Peninsula and
Greater Williamsburg
Building Partner

Contents

Preface

When my daughters were 2 and 4, I became a single mom. It was a devastating blow in my life. Although I know it happens to many, I didn't see it coming—it blindsided me both emotionally and financially. With a large property and house and a business of my own, my husband and I had bitten off more than we could chew. Together we were struggling financially, but separately we didn't have a prayer of keeping up.

Ignoring the bills works only up to a point, and one midwinter day, the electricity was cut off. Two days later, I was out of heating oil. Luckily, we had a woodstove that would keep the house warm (as long as I got up through the night to keep it burning). It was a horrifying episode in my life.

It was during this time that I made a solemn vow to myself: my kids would never be left as financially unprepared as I was. I would teach them about money—how to respect it, spend it, save it, and *earn* it. At that point, I hadn't a clue how to do this, or even whether

I was the right person for the job. After all, having put myself in such an awkward financial position, who was *I* to teach my kids about managing money?

I searched through many books and read any that seemed pertinent to my family's situation. Then we sat down and had a family meeting. I explained to them that Mommy was going to make sure they had everything they needed: clothes, food, a warm house, and even trips to fun places. I also explained that if they wanted to get extra things, they were going to be able to start earning their own money so they could get those things on their own. And I let them know this in a way that was exciting and something to look forward to.

I also let them know that Mommy was just one person and that this house was a big place and that I needed their help keeping it clean and doing some chores outside.

We talked about how they were going to be able to start earning money right here at home. They helped me come up with a list of things they could do around the house. Caitlyn was just 2 years old, and Ashley was just 4, but they were eager to help and earn some money. More than once it brought me to tears realizing just what amazing kids I had. And even now, as looking back to that time, I have tears—the good kind—rolling down my face. I had big hopes for new beginnings and a new relationship with my daughters as a single mom. I remember blasting the music and even busting some dance moves as we cleaned up toys, vacuumed, or swept, each doing our own chore or working together. We had a lot of fun.

Our system was a little different back then. I had a set of poker chips that I never used. So when they completed their chores and their behavior was good (we had a checklist that we went over each night) they got a chance to choose a white, red, or blue poker chip. Each chip represented something different: white was for candy, blue was for books, and red was for toys. They could also choose not to get a poker chip and instead have late bedtime, tickle time, or a variety of other rewards that they helped me come up with. These are some of the best memories I have. Usually, my kids would both pick tickle time. Now, this may not be quite what you're thinking. You see, *I* was the subject of the tickling. I am famously ticklish, and they are VERY good at tickling. So they would get three minutes to tickle me—*each*. One would hold my arms up and the other would tickle, and if I couldn't breathe, they had to pause. We had a blast, usually with them laughing even more than I did.

They learned several things with the poker chip system. One, they learned that they had choice. Two, they learned that it was not just about the money—often they would pick one of the rewards instead of the money. Three, they learned to be patient and save for an important item. When saving up for a toy or a book, they could count how many days they needed to save to have enough money to get their toy. As an added benefit (to me), they would normally be on their best behavior for the days needed to get what they were saving for. When they had enough chips they turned them in for cash, and we went shopping.

I remember one of the first big items that Caitlyn saved for was a beautiful stuffed bear at a country market. My daughter wanted it *so-o-o* badly. We talked about how much it cost, and she was still about three weeks away from having it. She was worried that it wouldn't be there when she had all the money saved up. I prepared her by saying that could be, but if it wasn't there, she would still have all that money saved up for the next great thing she found. Giving me a cute but nervous smile, she grabbed my hand, and we walked away and left the bear there. Three weeks later, she had earned all the money, and we went back. I was thrilled for Caitlyn when we walked into the store and found it still sitting on the shelf, waiting for her. She was so excited, she picked up the bear and gave it a big, long bear hug. She then proceeded to the cash register with it and handed the woman her hard-earned money. The cashier had no idea how important this moment was for my Caitlyn. This bear was a prized possession for some time. And it still sits in her closet with several other special teddy bears.

Saving for a Teddy Bear

The girls set up a Kool-Aid stand at the horse shows I hosted at the barn. This was a perfect time to peek in and see what their natural talents were. Ashley was measuring carefully, pouring drinks, collecting money. Caitlyn was taking cups of Kool-Aid with her to the spectators and direct-selling. She also took orders for more and brought them back to the arena. They were around 4 and 6 years old when they started this enterprise. I can still hear them calling out to the crowd, "Kool-Aid for sale, fifty cents a glass. Do you want blueberry or cherry"? Seriously, too cute for words!

When they were 7 and 9 they got their first bunny rabbits. Both females, right? Not! So a few weeks later, they had their first baby bunnies. These they sold to classmates and friends. The next litter was tougher to sell. So they went to the pet store, where they learned about the difference between wholesale and retail. That was also where they decided that they needed to find a way to sell the bunnies on their own if they wanted to make any money.

Then Ashley and Caitlyn came to T. Harv Eker's Millionaire Mind Seminar, and after a twelve- or fourteen-hour day, they were sitting in the back of the car on the way home, at eleven at night, talking about how many bunnies they needed in order to make a certain amount of passive income. They were eager to expand. I was grinning from ear to ear as I drove along.

By this time, my girls had already been using the money management system for some time. So now their focus was on simply creating a business name and expanding. The next morning on the drive in to the seminar, they were working away, writing things down. When we got to the seminar I found out that they were creating business names. They showed me, had me pick the three names I liked best, then went around to all the friends who were with us, and got their top three. Then they went off and asked participants at the seminar. When they finally had it narrowed down to just three names they talked to the seminar leader, who helped them tie in one as the name and one of the others as the tag line. And that was the genesis of "Bunnyville, where happiness comes a-hoppin'."

Seven years later, using the money management system in their business, they have expanded and have a retail division of their company. Ashley and Caitlyn now offer new cages, grooming supplies, treats, and bunny food. So when a family comes to get their bunny, they can get everything they need to set the bunny up at home, all in one place. They have about fifteen breeding bunnies and have zero debt. Can you imagine running a business for seven years and having *no debt*? They do all their own advertising, appointments, cleaning, Facebook fan page, recordkeeping, and everything it takes to own a bunny business. They also show their bunnies each year at the Royal Winter Fair in Toronto and bring home a slew of ribbons and trophies.

This alone is enough to make a mother proud. But during all this time, both girls were developing other talents. Ashley is a talented author (published five times), and Caitlyn is a talented and twice-published poet. The two girls are working together now, creating a how-to-care-for-your-bunny book, which they plan to sell online.

Ashley is an amazing young lady. She is also working on a book of short stories. I like to say that she has the ability to take you on an emotional journey that you were not expecting. Indeed, her success as a writer has been one of my main inspirations for writing this book. She is also three-quarters of the way into a sci-fi novel that she is excited about publishing. Ashley is 16.

I am not going through the typical teenage problems with either of my girls. I think much of the reason for this is what they learned and focused on as they were growing up. Rather than blame their actions on what the world is doing to them, they see how their own actions create their world.

Caitlyn is the kind of girl who feels everything. She sees the injustice in the world and wants to do something about it, sees a sad face and wants to put a smile on it. So what did she do with a portion of her earnings? Dedicated it to charity, of course, and went out and bought food for a struggling family. She is constantly doing what she can to raise money for those in need.

When my girls were 13 and 15, I sent them with a group to Jamaica to help in an orphanage and study with a group of spiritual leaders. Caitlyn was amazed at how these kids, who really had nothing, could be so happy. When she got back to the resort, she went up onstage in front of everyone who was waiting for the evening performance, and told them what she was doing. She asked for their help, and right away she had people bringing her money, which she and Ashley then took to the orphanage.

The money management system that I taught the girls and that I share in this book is my interpretation of what I learned at the T. Harv Eker Millionaire Mind Seminar—something I recommend that *everyone* attend. See the back of the book on how to get your free tickets.

I loved having conversations about how much something cost, how much we saved when we got things on sale, what we needed versus what we wanted. We also had many conversations about the commercials on TV, whether the products they touted were really worth spending money on, and whether the products really did what the ads claimed.

This is the kind of conversation that helps kids develop their sense around money and helps them see through the barrage of TV and other media telling them to buy more, throw it away and replace it with the newer, niftier model, and do the whole shebang on credit.

The idea for this book came when I was in Los Angeles, at a Peak Potential seminar on marketing. I was there learning what I could to enhance my horse business, and in the midst of an exercise, the thought for this book popped into my head. I knew in that very instant that it was the right path for me.

Looking at everything I had learned and experimented with in raising my girls, seeing them blossom as their confidence grew and their entrepreneurial creativity expanded, I knew that this was something I needed to share with the world. Far too many people struggle financially simply because no one ever showed them any kind of money management system.

Just this morning, at a secluded retreat setting, I was in charge of feeding the fish. Big bass, about ten of the biggest ones in the pond, were hanging out at the dock as usual, waiting for the food. Seeing those big lunkers sitting there in the water, I decided that since the little fish were getting ripped off, I was going to go to the other side of the pond and throw some food in there. Fish came nosing around, but no one ate. Could it be that they didn't recognize it as food, because they hadn't been exposed to it, since the big fish always got to it first? Is it the same with our kids? Are they missing opportunities because they don't recognize them when they see them? For the next few days, I'm going to keep feeding the younger, smaller fish. Today one of the bigger fish came by and took one of the pieces of fish food. Maybe the younger ones will see this and know what to do. I hope so, just as I hope this book will help you recognize, and then show your child, all the amazing opportunities that are out there, just waiting for them.

My goal—and yes, I know it's a grand one—is to change the world. Let's send our kids into the world with skills and confidence so that they can create their own income whenever they need to, and so that when they have money in their hands they will know how to manage it to give them the best chance of success.

I am excited about sharing this with you and your family, and I can't wait to hear the stories of how this knowledge has transformed both you and your children.

Acknowledgments

My deepest thanks go out to the friends and family who supported me in making this book, from concept to creation, and everything in between.

I also thank my parents for teaching by example and showing me how to work hard, stick with it, and be determined enough not only to open the doors that were in front of me but also to step through them and turn my dreams into reality.

Most importantly, I would like to thank my daughters, Ashley and Caitlyn. It is because of them that you can now hold this book in your hands.

I am blessed to have the most amazing daughters a mother could ask for. Not only did they take to each step of learning about money and business, but they developed their own ideas and ran with them. Truly, they inspire me.

Chapter 1

Welcome to the Lemonade Stand

"**L**emonade for sale, fifty cents a glass!"

Do you remember your first sale? How about the pleasant jingle of change at the end of the day, or the lessons learned from picking a bad business location? The opportunities from such a simple and fun experience for your children can teach them a wealth of skills, including planning, goal setting, communication skills, money management, and more.

But what if this is just the start for your budding young entrepreneur? What if they want to continue earning their own money—continue to feel that sense of pride at doing something they love and being financially rewarded for it?

Though it may not look like it, today's society is bursting with amazing opportunities available to your child. This book is designed to help parents guide their kids on the road to success in business and in life. Whether it's a summer project or the beginnings of lifelong entrepreneurship, what your child

The Road to Success

can learn with this book will set the stage for a lifetime of success stories.

Just as important as the learning is the discovery that they have control over their income. Chapter 4 provides a simple money management system that is useful whether your child decides to start a business or not. Using money from birthdays, Christmas, or house chores, kids (and their parents) will learn how to set aside money for spending, saving, investing, and giving. Setting up habits now that keep them out of impulse buying will prevent them from ever getting on the paycheck-to-paycheck treadmill.

It's up to us to show kids how to build wealth and be financially intelligent, because our schools are definitely *not* teaching them about it in the classroom.

I have seen firsthand the value of supporting a child's dream. I have seen my two girls flourish, learning skills and lessons that will stay with them for a lifetime. They started learning about money management at ages 2 and 4 and started their own business when they were 7 and 9, and now, 7 years later, they are still growing that business.

Most of us were never taught in school about spending, saving, investing, and giving to charity. These subjects have always been left up to parents or employers, or else just left for kids to figure out on their own (usually through TV and other media). This gap in learning the ins and outs of financial matters is plaguing us as a society. As indebtedness (both individually and nationally) keeps growing, media such as commercials and movies glorify credit cards and "pay nothing for a year" purchases. Financial debt is the *number one* reason for stress. It is also the leading cause of suicide, and one of the biggest factors in divorce.

Debt creates a society of people who are enslaved by their jobs and unable to enjoy what we were put on earth to do: to connect, have fun, and create a better world. Many people work overtime or take on a second job and still struggle to make ends meet. Money management is one of the most important and, in truth, *easiest* things you can teach your children—and one that will have a massive impact on their financial well-being in their adult life. When we are all personally in better financial positions we are able to contribute to our world on a different level and improve the quality of our lives.

What could you do for your family, community, country, or world if you didn't have to worry about money? People often fantasize about a perfect world where young children are brought up to learn concepts that will enable them to do great things for themselves and others. But what if we didn't need a perfect world to create this way of being? What if we were to decide to start creating a world *right now* for ourselves and our children that would support them on a successful road ahead? Imagine the tremendous impact this could have on the world and on the issues that cause conflict from a global level right down to the personal level. If enough parents were to decide to teach their children the ways of financial success, we might even change the world as we know it!

So as your kids embark on this journey of wonder and fulfillment, feel free to take it with them—in fact, I recommend it. Kids are more likely to follow with you, their parents, as a role model. Seeing you display the same financial habits you are teaching them will only encourage them to adopt those habits as their own. Remember the adage "it's not what you say but what you do." So fill out your own charts, and dream about what you would truly love to do. Perhaps you, too, can start your own small business. Remember, what you focus on expands, so do the exercises with your kids, and enjoy the journey.

It is vitally important to teach kids early about money—spending it, saving it, investing it, and giving it. Now is the time to make this way for kids to look at money the new normal. I have also seen the pride they take in earning and managing their own money—learning a skill that I know is setting them up for life.

Chapter 2

How to Use This Book

This book is set up as a guide for parents to start conversations about money with their kids. It can be used for any age. I started when my kids were 2 and 4, but I've seen many start at later ages, with wonderful results.

In using this book, one of the most important things to remember is that you are setting up conversations, not just telling your kids what to do and how to do it. For the information within these pages to be most effective, it has to be highly interactive between you and your kids.

Make sure you really listen to what they have to say. They will reveal many things to you "between their words." Allow them to explore and ask questions. Let them make mistakes and learn from them. What better way to learn about handling challenges and disappointments, as well as success, than with you standing by to support, encourage, and guide them in taking their next step? The hidden beauty of this is that you, too, are learning at the same time.

Each chapter contains both information and exercises for your child. It's important to read each chapter fully, or share the reading, and then complete the exercises before moving to the next chapter.

It may take an hour or a week to complete each chapter, depending on the time dedicated to it. There is NO RUSH. It's more important that you make it a fun experience for the family and that your children understand that they are taking steps to create an amazing future.

Depending on your child's age and interest, they may get only as far as the chapter on their first job and stay there several weeks, even months. No problem. You can finish reading the book on your own and let your kids know that when they're ready to make more money, they just need to say so and you can continue with the following chapters.

Not every child will want to start their own business, and that is definitely okay. It is critical, though, that the child *understand* the money management concepts and divide their money into the different jars. This will set them up with skills and habits that make the difference between a life of financial struggle and a balanced way of thinking about and handling money.

You and your child can read the chapter with the interviews one interview at a time or straight through, at any time during your journey. It shows what a wide range of young people, with different life circumstances and different driving goals, have done.

When your kids are ready to venture into self-employment enjoy the chapters that take them through the process. Again, it must be fun and interactive. If you have small-business ideas that you've been thinking about, play along with the exercises. Many multimillion-dollar businesses started with a simple idea.

I want to take a moment to thank you for getting this book for your family. You have just given your children a huge gift: the opportunity to have a successful, rewarding life without ever letting money become one of the stressors they will need to face. The time you spend now will pay off massively in their future.

Enjoy the journey.

Chapter 3

The Mind-set of Financial Success

The power of our mind is vastly underrated. Our thoughts and words shape the way we feel. If we're thinking about the ill-mannered driver who cut us off in traffic, we are feeling angry; if we're thinking about playing with a puppy, we feel happy and carefree. Our brain doesn't know the difference between a thought and reality, so if we're thinking about events or actions that make us angry or upset, we are just feeding our mind and body with negativity.

It's hard to be resourceful when we are upset. Have you ever had an argument in your head about something you thought *might* happen? I have interrupted myself on many occasions (including just this morning) when I caught myself getting really upset about conversations in my head—conversations that weren't even happening anywhere else! Most of the time, this movie we have playing in our heads just gets us in trouble. If this topic does come up for real later on, I will need to watch and gauge my reactions so

I don't refer back to how *I thought* they might react, and instead keep my focus on how they *really are* reacting in the moment. We are free to choose the movies that play in our head, free to be the creator and director. So be watchful of your thoughts and how they make you feel.

How you feel will play a large part in determining your actions. Say, for example, your child does something wonderful and you've had a great day. You may decide to read them an extra story before bed. If you've had a tough, really gnarly day, you may just send them to bed early because of how your day made you feel (or the way you *interpreted,* and perhaps held on to, that negative energy).

Anything you do has a consequence or result. So if my desired result is to make a lot of money, yet I sit on the couch watching movies all day, I will never reach my goal. But if I want to make an extra thousand dollars this month and I get up each morning excited about that result and spend my day doing what I need to create it, then I have a much better chance of receiving it.

So we want to teach our kids about how the *thoughts* they entertain create the *feelings* they experience, which will determine the *actions* they take and, finally, the *results* they get. It's up to us to help them let go of the negative thoughts and beliefs and look through the cloud to its silver lining. That is how we help propel them forward in business and in life.

I can't tell you how many times over the years I would catch my kids wasting their energy by dwelling on the negative, and direct them to find a solution. So imagine my shock and delight when, on several occasions, I found myself in a sad or frustrated state about something, my kids would say, "Okay, Mom, what can you do to make this situation better? And often, the mere fact that they had noticed and were able to say that to me was enough to start turning my attitude around. I have also witnessed them catching themselves and rephrasing or changing their thoughts in mid sentence.

What your kids think about money and getting rich will be a huge factor in their success. If they think rich people are crooks or selfish misers with no friends, their chances of getting rich are going to be fairly slim. After all, why would they want to become that kind of person? But if they think rich people are creative and thoughtful and help people in the world and go to lots of great places and don't have to worry about money, then of course they want to be this kind of person!

So let's find out what your kids think about what it takes to get rich. What does a person have to do to become rich? Give at least five actions below.

_____

_____

_____

_____

_____

If you find a negative meaning or attitude in any of the above answers, you may want to help them look at it in a more positive way or break that myth if it is untrue.

Your kids must first think it's *possible* for them to get rich, start a business, or do whatever they are gearing up to do. In today's world, they can make it happen if they create a solid plan and then work toward it.

A vitally important key for your kids' business is that they set their goals and then do the things they need to do to accomplish those goals.

Rich People, good or bad

Do your kids want to make a lot of money? And if so, do they want to because it's something they *like* to do? Is it because they want to help people make themselves and others happy? It's crucially important that there be a strong reason driving them. Maybe there is a specific toy they want to save up for, or a new bike—some goal they will move toward that can serve as a good starting point. Maybe they want to make money to help a good cause. It must be something that will drive them to succeed when they are learning to manage money and to work at their new business.

So what is financial success? Everyone is going to have their own definition. Find out how your child defines it. Ask them what would be a lot of money. Write their answer down here. _____ _____ What is it that they would want to use their money for? Get your kids thinking about these things for themselves. And remember, it's okay to go crazy and think big. Also get them to think about what they can do for other people. Let them go crazy with the ideas. Let their imaginations soar, and keep in mind that the desire to help others with a particular problem has sparked ideas that made many a fortune. When they've decided what their definition of financial success is, then you'll have a good sense of the lifestyle they want to lead. Direct them and guide them to a bigger picture than the one that includes just themselves.

One definition of "financial freedom" is "the ability to live the lifestyle that you desire, without working or having to rely on anyone else for money." So here are some more questions to ask your kids: What would you do with your money? What would you do with your free time? What would you do to help this world? This mind-set is what will ultimately empower you and your kids to achieve great success.

It's really important to look at our way of thinking about money and finances. Are you coming from a place of scarcity, or are you coming from a place of abundance?

Let's say you're with your son or your daughter at the store, and you see something you really like. The first thing that you say is "I can't afford that," or "we can't get that right now," even though they know you want it. Your kids see your actions, and by saying "I can't afford it," you create a mind-set of scarcity that affects them just as much as it affects you.

So an attitude of abundance might sound like this: "I really love that couch, and I wonder what we could do so we can get it." "I wonder where we might be able to make some extra money." Or "If we save up, we can get that in about three months." You always have a choice. You can either discuss ways that you can get the couch later (abundance mind-set), or talk about all the reasons why you can't have it (scarcity mind-set). Now, you may find another, less expensive couch that will work, or you may decide that you would rather spend your money elsewhere, but that doesn't mean you must see yourself as a victim of your circumstances or lapse into a mentality of scarcity.

What happens when your kids want something at the store? An attitude of scarcity says, "You don't need that," or "It's too much money," or "We [you] can't afford that! Who do you think we are, the Rockefellers?" And the list goes on.

An attitude of abundance would sound quite different—maybe more like this: "Wow, that is a great-looking toy! What account would you pay for it out of? Oh, right, the 'Play' jar. How much do you have in your 'Play' jar? Okay, that means you still need how much money if you want to buy this? Just five dollars more to save—that's exciting! How do you think you can save that extra five dollars?" Notice how this is more of an investigation of *how* to get the money than a list of all the reasons why they can't. Then, if they decide it's too much money to spend on that item, they can change their mind. But—and this is key—they have changed their mind because they want to use their money for something with more value, not because they can't afford the thing they want.

Remember that what you do, say, and believe about money has a profound influence on your children. Make sure you are setting a good example, by believing in their dreams and yours, and believing in their ability to fashion reality from their dreams. Let them know that you fully expect them to reach for their dreams and do whatever it takes to achieve what they want to achieve. It starts with you, so it's imperative that you have that can-do attitude about yourself, and believe that they can do it, too.

It's vitally important that your kids dream and set goals. Do the following exercise with your kids. Then share with each other afterward.

Dreams Exercise

1. Set a timer for five minutes.
2. Brainstorm on paper *everything* your child has ever wanted. If they are too young to write, you can write it for them. Remember, there are NO LIMITS. Do they want to travel, have a cottage, own an island, drive a Lamborghini, start a nonprofit organization, and feed a thousand famine-stricken children in Africa? Be specific!
3. When the timer goes off, stop. Next, beside each wish, write down when they want to have it. In a year? Five years? Ten?
4. Have them pick their top three one-year goals. Put these on a separate piece of paper and hang it on the wall where they can see it every day. My kids have also created vision boards of the big things they wanted in life, from pictures they drew or found in magazines.

Running their business gets a lot more exciting when they have goals on how much they want to make in a month, how many widgets they want to sell in a weekend, or how many followers they want to get on their fan page. I like to have yearly, monthly, and weekly goals.

When setting goals, it's important to be specific. That means, on your child's list (and on yours, too) of top three one-year goals, make sure the date on it is one year from today. Also, make sure that the goal listed is measurable. Not "I want to make a lot of money," but "I want to earn a thousand dollars this year in my new business," or "I want to read five new books this year."

The next part is making sure they know their reason for setting the goal. Say they want to make X amount of money. Is that because it's something they love to do? Because they want to make people happy? Because they want that cool new bicycle? Or so they can tell all their friends? It's essential that they have a strong reason driving them.

Having a good starting goal and a compelling reason for achieving it will help drive them to succeed in their new business. That *driving reason* for their goal is the fuel that feeds their fire.

Chapter Discussions

1. Ask your children why they want to make money.
2. Find out what they think financial success means.
3. Talk about what they could do with the money they make, both immediately and over the long term, for themselves and for others.
4. Ask them whom could they help if they had a lot of money.
5. Work with them in deciding what they want to accomplish in the next week, month, and year.

Chapter 4

Teaching Your Kids How to Handle Money

It's one thing to teach your kids how to start making money, but it is just as important—perhaps even more so—to teach them what to do with their money once they have it.

Very often, parents wait until their kids are in their teens before encouraging them to start making their own money, and very few parents actually teach their kids how to save, spend, invest, and give. And why would they, when most parents aren't even learning that for themselves? Our education system doesn't include basic money management. Our kids may learn how to count change and total up the cost of several items in a shopping cart, but that doesn't go very far when they grow up and need to pay rent, buy groceries, and cover the many other expenses in life.

When I started teaching money management to my 4-year-old and my 2-year–old, maybe they were too young to really understand what was happening. But over time, the language of moneymaking and money management became as clear to them as how to walk and talk. As they grew up, they continued to handle and manage their own money.

Many people who are dead broke and heavily in debt today are not that way because they didn't make enough money, but because they mismanaged or threw away too much of it. I used to ride a huge financial roller coaster and have at many times had an abundance of cash available to me. I saw that as an opportunity to go on vacation or buy a new TV, never thinking that I could be setting some aside for leaner times. That pattern really started when I was a kid. I remember getting five dollars from my dad and going to the corner store as quickly as I could to spend every cent on candy. Unfortunately, as I grew up my spending habits never changed—the things I was spending on just got bigger. Even worse, soon I could get my hands on credit cards, so I was not just blowing the money I had in my hands, but going deep into debt with the "convenience" of credit cards. This is why it's critical to teach kids good money habits from the moment they start to experience money for themselves.

I certainly do not blame my parents for my financial decisions. I do know, however, that much of what I learned about spending money, I learned by watching my parents spend their money. But today our kids don't learn just by observing their parents; now the media are a huge factor in our kids' education. And unfortunately, the media glorify credit cards, buying for immediate gratification, taking out loans to get what you want, and credit-buying programs that let you go for a year before making the first payment—a true recipe for burdensome financial debt. This means that we as parents need to have an even stronger influence so our kids don't get caught in that trap. They are also being influenced by their friends, some of whom get money handed to them whenever they want it, and thus never learn to respect it. Others, who don't get enough, develop resentful attitudes toward money.

Exercise: Take a few minutes and ask your kids to tell you about their money habits (if they are handling money already). Do they like to spend it all right away? Do they save it? Do they give some to others? If they are not handling their own money yet, ask them what they know about money, and write it below.

_____

_____

_____

_____

_____

Now, parents, what are some spending habits you had as a kid? Do you still have that habit now, or has it changed?

_____

_____

_____

_____

_____

How do we help our kids avoid the financial traps that so many are caught in, and instead help them build a solid foundation that will lead them to a life of financial abundance? We first need to identify how they (and we as parents) habitually manage money, to determine our starting place. If you have a very young child, this may not apply. I would, however, highly encourage every parent to examine their own spending style so they can understand the kind of influence they are having on their kids. Your spending style is the basic way you handle your own money—how you spend or save as well as how you handle bills. We can divide ourselves into four basic spending styles; spender, saver, monk, or avoider. I'll explain what those categories mean in just a moment.

It's important to have balance in our spending habits. Too much weight in the "spender" category means you have no money left to pay bills or save for a rainy day. Too much weight in the "saver" category means you don't get to enjoy the fruits of your labor and may begin to resent money. The avoider gets into financial trouble by ignoring the bills (usually because there is no money to pay them), and the monk feels that it is "unspiritual" to have money. (Of course, that argument has a hole in it, because if we have an abundance of money, just think of all the great things we can do with it to help others.)

Once you decide your spending "style," it's important to determine whether it is serving you. It really is all about balance. Understanding your spending pattern will help you see what you need to do to balance out the categories. It's okay to spend money. In fact, it's important to go out and treat yourself and have fun with 10 percent of your income. (We'll talk more about balance in later chapters.)

If your kids are old enough to be handling and spending money, you can see whether they blow it all at once, as I did (spender), hide it in a box or the bank for a rainy day (saver), or want to give it to those in greater need (monk). You won't see many kids who are avoiders—that usually shows up when the bills do.

Most people think that to become financially free, they need a really big income. But this is not the case. With a good money management system, you can build your wealth very quickly.

Spending Styles

For a chart on money savings over time, see appendix A in the back of the book.

Also, being financially free doesn't mean you have to be rich. It simply means that you have enough money in savings and investments to maintain the lifestyle you desire without needing to work (or working very little).

Take a moment and look back on your dream list and your top three goals. Keep those dreams and goals in your thoughts every day, and keep the attitude that this is something you are working toward. What we focus on expands. So keep your eyes on the target as you step forward with this process.

Setting kids up with a system will help them develop habits to create, at the very minimum, a stable financial foundation. Or they could become fabulously rich and be able to have a life that lets them focus on what is truly important to them instead of working sixty hours a week just to make ends meet.

So here we go. The following is a system I learned at my very first Millionaire Mind Intensive seminar with T. Harv Eker. This is a seminar I highly recommend to both adults and kids. My kids went for the first time when they were 9 and 11. To get access to this amazing three-day seminar (value over $1,200 per seat), check the back of the book to find out how to register for your FREE TICKETS.

There may be some things I do slightly differently from the way T. Harv Eker teaches. This is my interpretation of this great system. It has worked amazingly well both for me and for my kids.

The first step is to get your kids five jars or containers that they can put their money in—preferably see-through containers so they can always see what they have inside. I like to call them "freedom jars." Get some sparkles, stickers, paint, or something that your child can use to decorate a label on each jar. Label them "Play," "Learning," "Wealth," "Angel," and "Plan." (Mom and Dad, if you're playing along, you will also need a jar labeled "Necessities.") Then, when the jars are labeled and decorated, have the kids put them somewhere they will see them every day.

When your kids get their first paycheck, allowance, or birthday or Christmas money, you will sit down with them and a calculator in front of their jars. I suggest that they divide their money in the following proportions:

- Play jar 20%
- Learning jar 20%
- Long-term savings jar 20%
- Wealth jar 30%
- Angel jar 10%

*Get a calculator you can dedicate just for these calculations—one with an easy "%" button.

- **Play**: This is the jar that your kids will have the most fun with. This is the one that they get to spend on ANYTHING THEY WANT, so Mom and Dad must be careful here. If the kids want to spend it all on a toy, let them. This is not the time to be practical. This is the time to play, enjoy, dream, and spend their money guilt free. One rule is that this money must be spent fully every thirty to sixty days. They are not allowed to save this money for a bigger toy (there is a place for this). They must find something to do with this money, to enjoy it right away. It can be a thing or an experience. This is important because they learn to treat themselves and learn that they deserve to have fun and enjoy money.

- **Learning**: This is for anything that will teach them something. My Ashley loves to read, so much of her "learning" money went into buying books. It could go toward lessons they want to take—maybe a photography workshop or a special course at school. Now, if you were planning on getting them in hockey anyway, I wouldn't

Learning the Jar System

recommend asking them to pay for the lessons, but if they want additional lessons above what you either plan to do or can afford, this is the jar where they can start saving for them.

- **Plan**: This is the category where your kids can stash away funds for bigger-ticket items, such as a new computer game, a computer, or even a bike—something that will take some time to save up for. It's a good idea to help your kids think about something they want to save for, because it helps to have something to look forward to and work toward. They can even get a picture of it and put it somewhere they will see it every day.

- **Wealth**: This is the jar where they start building their wealth. Let your kids know that they will never, *ever* spend money from this category. This is where they can invest in a registered education savings plan, stocks, or silver and gold. (I bought actual silver coins with my kids' wealth money when they were 11 and 13.) Kids will require help from their parents in choosing wise ways to get their money working for them. If an investment is ever sold, the money from the investment is to be reinvested in something else. This is their golden goose (or "golden pony," as I like to call it) that will take care of them in their retirement. The interest earned in this category gets reinvested, too, to help their wealth grow even faster. If I had thought about this category when I was a kid, I would never have had to worry about my retirement. (Nor would I have thought that retirement meant I had to work until I was 65.) This could enable your kids to retire early with a great lifestyle and spend their retirement doing the things they really love.

- **Angel**: This category is for charities or giving in any way that will help those in need. When my kids first started putting money aside to give to charities, I had no idea where it would lead or what they would learn. This teaches your kids to look outside themselves to see others in need. It gives them an opportunity to make a difference, and what a perfect time to start, when there are no huge bills towering above their heads! My Caitlyn would come home from school with forms, collecting for various charities, and ask me to donate. Then she would go to her room and bring out five dollars, or twenty-five, to add to the donation herself. If it was a charity that really touched her, she would donate more. One Christmas season, she took her "angel" money to the store and bought groceries for a needy family. Ashley would save hers and send a bigger chunk to World Wildlife Fund, because that was a charity close to her heart. She even decided to set up a fund-raiser at an event that I was holding at the barn. This was such an amazing experience for Ashley because she is a very shy girl, and I let her know that it was a great idea. I also told her she needed to call World Wildlife Fund and find out how to set it up and what they could do to support her. Together we found the phone number, and we talked about who she needed to talk to and what kind of questions to ask, and then I just sat back and watched her fight this fear of the unknown as she made the call. She did a terrific job. That year they made around two hundred dollars. Other years they made over five hundred. Your kids could donate to the local food bank or to anything that makes them feel good. It's a wonderful habit to get your kids started with.

The percentages given above for the contributions to each jar are simply a guideline—feel free to play with them. I have found, however, that these percentages are a great balance and have shown excellent results for many people.

You'll notice that in the adult section below, we've added a jar labeled "Necessities." Until your child needs to start paying rent, groceries, and so on, let them put more into the other categories.

Before you ship them off to college or university, though, make sure the necessities category is added in. It's a great idea to have at least three months of expenses saved up before they go out on their own, so they may want to add a necessities jar at least six months to a year before they move away. This will also get them used to the change in the spending money they have available.

Help them figure out how to do this breakdown on the calculator. With the younger kids, you may have to help them each time. Perhaps they can push the buttons or write something down, or help count out the money. Let them do as much as they can. As an added bonus for the younger kids, they will get a head start on understanding the basics of percentages before they even get to it in math class.

When they are dividing the money, celebrate when they get it all into their jars. To keep track, I also write down when I deposit and withdraw money from the jars. You'll find sample forms in the back of the book for tracking the money. See Money Tracking Charts, appendix B. As an adult, I follow the same system, but my categories and percentages are slightly different.

Any incoming money that I receive is divided up into the following categories. This includes paychecks, birthday money, money I find on the street. *Any* money that comes into my hands is divided into these categories. Now, parents, if you find that your bills are too high to divide your entire pay, take whatever you can from your incoming money, even if it's twenty dollars, or five dollars, out of your paycheck, and divide it. It's about creating the habit, and the amount you can divide will grow, especially as you see the results.

The additional jar you see here is the "Necessities" jar. This one is for rent or mortgage, car payments, food, gas, water, bills, clothing—whatever you need to buy. So here are the jars:

- Necessities 55%
- Play 10%
- Long-term savings 10%
- Education 10%
- Wealth 10%
- Charity 5%

So there you have it. It's simple but not necessarily easy. This will require consistency from you and from your kids. The rewards are great. The hidden gem here is that just through the actions of tracking and separating the money into the various categories, you and your kids are creating the great habit of following through and keeping commitments.

Exercise: To complete the Freedom Jar Exercise, go to the appendixes. This will help your kids understand the process of dividing money into the various jars, or you can use real money to demonstrate. See appendix C, "The Cash Jars Exercise."

Also, depending on your child's age, the "What Goes Where" chart can be a useful tool. This will help your kids understand how to decide which jar is for what item. See appendix D, "What Goes Where."

To find out more details on this system by T. Harv Eker, check the references section for the Millionaire Mind book and seminar.

Bank Accounts

For myself, I set up this system both in the bank and with my jars on my bedroom dresser. So does this mean I have six bank accounts and my kids have five? Yes, exactly. I have one checking account and five high-interest savings accounts. Each bank will be different, but you will want one checking account that is your "Necessities" for adults, or "Play" for kids. I deposit all my money into that account and then transfer the money to the appropriate accounts online or at the bank. It's easy. The second account on my debit card is my "Play." For my book-loving daughter, it is her "Education." Set it up to suit your needs. Be sure to look at what activities are subject to bank charges. Most savings accounts do not have monthly charges but will have per-use charges. So determine the best accounts with the lowest bank charges.

I generally don't suggest bank accounts for kids until they have built up their money some. Having the actual cash visually in front of them is inspiring.

I watched my kids use the jar system in their business. (They had slightly different categories—we'll talk about that in a later chapter.) They gave themselves a paycheck from their business income and went on to divide their money into their personal jars. I was amazed at how it paid off. They were able to buy things for their business when an opportunity came up, because the money was in their savings, ready for just such an opportunity. After coaching and helping and watching them for several years, I finally started to do this for myself. It seemed that all of a sudden, I had money available to get that new stereo system I had wanted for so long. I had also saved up enough money to start investing in the stock market. What worked for my daughters was working for their mom, too!

Chapter 5

Their First Job:
Start at Home

From a very early age, my kids had responsibilities around the house. When they were 2 and 4 years old they were responsible for making their bed every day, bringing their dishes from the table to the sink (I washed and dried), putting away their own toys, and various other tasks.

One of the biggest challenges facing parents today happens because they do so much for their children in the early years and then, when the kid is 10 to 15, they change the rules. No wonder the kid puts up so much resistance to helping out around the house!

Kids who have everything done for them are at a real disadvantage when the time comes to learn to do things on their own. Starting them young with simple things will set them up with a pattern of doing well, figuring things out, and being successful. It also gives them a sense of belonging in the family, and the feeling that their contribution makes a difference. Of course, the tasks will need to be age appropriate. You won't be asking your 4-year-old to shovel the driveway, but they can come out with a toy shovel and "help" while you work away at it. And kids can make beds, sweep or vacuum, wash floors, clean windows, do dishes, and more.

If your kids are already in their teens or preteens, don't worry, you can still get started with this system. You just have to make sure they see the benefits for themselves in this, as well as the fact that they have a responsibility to the family to do their share. So what are the benefits to your kids? Here's the biggest one: they get paid for their work!

What worked so well in my family can work for yours, too. Sit down with your child(ren) and make a list of the things they feel they can do around the house to help out. To complete the sense of contribution and responsibility, it's important that they feel involved. Bringing them in on deciding which chores to do also helps *you* understand what things they like to do, what they are worried about not being able to do well, and what they don't want to do.

Once you've come up with a list, you will look at all the items and decide which ones to include in daily responsibilities, weekly responsibilities and monthly responsibilities. You will ask your child if this feels like a doable list. Then I would suggest that you put it in writing and have them sign it, to indicate that they are committed to doing these tasks. See the sample contract in appendix E.

Coming up with the "allowance" is your next step. Personally, I like to call it a paycheck rather than an allowance so that they realize that if they don't complete their tasks, they don't get paid, period. It may sound harsh, but hey, if you did nothing at your job, you wouldn't be surprised if your boss fired you or didn't pay you. I don't give half pay if half the work is done. If they do not complete 100 percent of the work, they don't get paid. This is preparing them for the real world on several levels. On the daily small activities, I

Creating a Chore list

generally let them do just five days out of the seven, especially if we had outings or company.

The first time my kids didn't complete their chores, they were shocked and angry—*outraged*, now that I think of it—when I refused to pay them. They must not have thought I was serious about the contract. Be sure to write this stipulation in your agreement that states what their weekly, monthly, or daily responsibilities are. That way, when this day comes (and I'm willing to bet that someday it will), you can pull out the contract, show them where they signed, and remind them what they agreed to. For my kids, this happened a few times before they got it all sorted out. Now that they are teenagers, I don't harangue them if they don't get all their tasks done—I simply don't pay them. When they want to have money again (from this source, anyway), they'll get their work done.

My kids generally get thirty dollars a month, but you'll work out what is fair, with your financial situation, for the time they spend and the tasks on their list. Make sure the paycheck is something you can afford. I typically paid my girls on the first of the month for the work done the previous month. We would calculate the weeks that their chores were done, and I would give them their paychecks. For example, thirty dollars for the month, divided by four weeks, equals seven and a half per week. If they completed all their work only three of the four weeks, then they got twenty-one dollars. You can track the chore completions on the family calendar or a simple chore calendar.

When my kids were very young I paid them daily, so they could get really jazzed about it and see immediate results. My system was a little different back then, but the same concept applied. Do what will work best for your family situation. Whether you pay out daily, weekly, or monthly is not the important part. Your consistency, and doing what you said you would do, is.

Getting started, there may be some tasks your kids don't know how to do yet, or need some help with at first. This is not a problem. They may need a few weeks' transition time before they have the skills to do their work, but that's okay—any new job requires a certain amount of on-the-job-training.

Now, Mom or Dad, if you happen to be a control freak, this won't be easy. For the first little while, perhaps a week or so, I would help my kids with new skills such as making their bed. At 2 and 4 years old, this was not something they knew how to do yet. We put music on, laughed, and made it like a game. I showed them how to do it, and then let them try. It didn't look as though I had made the bed. In fact, it was a rumpled mess. When we finally got the sheets and blankets straightened out, we celebrated. We danced and jumped up and down, and I told them what a great job they had done. Then came the parade of stuffed animals! My older daughter, Ashley, would spend the next half hour after I left the room, setting up her toys that slept there in the daytime. She had fun. It made her proud, and it was A-OK with me.

For the first part, when helping them make the bed, you can guide them with straightening out the sheets and blankets (but don't do it all for them). You can use suggestions such as "Hey, honey, come over here and give this corner a pull. Look how that made everything straight—isn't that great?" Remember to celebrate every little victory. This continuous positive reinforcement will build a sense of accomplishment and, over time, mastery.

Once they have the idea (this may take a week or it may take just a couple of days, depending on their age), prepare them for solo bed-making day (or whatever task you are training them to do). Take out a calendar and show them when they will start on their own. Let them know you're confident in them, that you know they can do it.

The next step is one of the most important. When they go to make their bed, let them do it on their own. Do not follow. Resist the urge to check on them. Let them call you when they're done. When they call you and you go into the room, make a big deal out of what a great job they did, no matter what it looks like! Be prepared—it may look like a battle zone. Who cares? Look back on the first time you did something new or difficult. It's how you start off that is most important. If you tell them what needs to be corrected, you'll take the wind out of their sails. But if you congratulate them and tell them how proud you are, they'll be excited to do it again tomorrow. Practice makes permanent.

The other *really* important thing at work here is that you are gently steering them away from perfectionism—a habit that is neither useful nor healthy. You are teaching them that what they

A Clean Room

did is great. They will naturally get better with practice and will always be proud of having done the best they could. They will also be doing what they can to improve their work. If, as they get older, you don't see much of an improvement, you can always go back in for a "refresher" training to upgrade the quality of their work. If you do need to do this, approach it with an attitude of *suggesting*. For example, you could say something to the effect of "this method seems to work really well for me, and I find it quicker and get even better results. What do you think?" Asking "What do you think?" keeps them involved and shows them that their thoughts matter to you.

So, from a very early age, you can teach your kids to start earning money around the house. Some people feel that kids should be responsible for certain chores and not be paid. If this is your belief, then simply list the paid and unpaid chores separately. Perhaps state in your agreement that unpaid AND paid chores must be done for them to receive their paycheck.

Home is a safe and loving environment for your kids to learn about earning money.

The Next Step

Once you've set up a routine with their chore schedule you may find that your child becomes interested in other ways to make money. This is when the concept of being their own boss can come into play. They may not be interested for some time. So you can always bring up the subject and see if they're interested. If they aren't, no big deal. Just plant the seed and let them know that whenever they are interested in making more money you have some interesting ideas for them.

You may find that if you go out shopping and they see something they would like to buy, you can talk about how much they need to save and how long it will take. This is also a great time to talk about how they could get extra money and buy it sooner if they had another source of income.

You can randomly talk about ways that other people make money in business, and ask what they think or even what sorts of things they may want to do.

Exercise

1. Sit down with your kids and create a list of chores they can do (dishes, sweeping, bed making, weeding and watering, trash).
2. Agree on daily, weekly, and monthly chores.
3. Decide on top tasks that will be on their regular list, and star these.
4. Decide on a "paycheck" amount and a pay schedule (daily, weekly, monthly).
5. Sign the agreement. (See the sample contract in appendix E.)

Chapter 6

A Job versus Self-Employment:

The Good, the Bad, and the Just Plain Horrendous

The choice between working for a living and starting your own business is a no-brainer for some, and a long, thought-provoking process for others. Below, I have listed a variety of points for and against each choice, for you and your child to think about.

The best way to use this chapter, as with many of the others, is to read it aloud together. Have an interactive discussion about what each of these terms means. Some of it may be over your child's head, but you'll be surprised at how much they do get. You may see a lightbulb go off as you're talking about how the two systems work. Remember, it isn't about trying to sway them either way. It is about having a totally open conversation about the pros and cons of both systems. Perhaps your child will add some great points of their own—if they do, add them to this page.

A way that may help your child distinguish is that house chores are like a job—you have a boss and get paid for the work you do, and there is a specific amount that you get paid from that job—no more and no less. You may have a great boss or a difficult boss (being a parent boss can be tough). Self-employment could be a lemonade stand that you put up in your neighborhood or on the corner of a busy park. You can pay a friend a few dollars to come out and sell lemonade while you stay home and play video games or read, and maybe make your whole monthly pay from house chores in just one day. Or you may only make a few dollars and not quite cover your expenses.

Job Vs Self Employed

Have fun talking about these points, and throw in some of your own as you talk about this with your child.

A Job

The Good

- Regular paycheck
- Fairly reliable income
- Leave your work behind when you come home
- May have benefits
- May be protected by a union
- Possibly regular hours
- Invest only the time between punching in and punching out
- Just show up and do what you were hired to do
- During weekends, forget about the job and just relax
- Can call in sick and still get paid, vacation pay
- Unemployment benefits
- Maternity leave
- Company annual bonus
- They take care of bookwork
- "Guaranteed" income

The Bad and the Horrendous

- No job security (can get fired or lose job easily)
- Wages limited to salary or hours worked (if hourly)
- Lull in sales means less pay (if pay is commission based)
- Cap on how much money you can make
- The benefit of your hard work goes to the company, not to you

- Have to get up when the alarm rings, even if you don't feel like it
- Can't choose your boss or coworkers
- You may be one of the many people who don't enjoy t heir job

Self-Employment

The Good
- Set your own hours
- No cap on how much money you can make
- Unlimited income
- No one can fire you
- Can take days off and holidays when you want
- Take as many vacations as you like (be careful here)
- Can have someone else manage operations and make you money when you're not there
- Can have someone do what you are not good at or don't like to do
- Vehicle, home office, and many everyday expenses are business write-offs (be careful not to go crazy—leave some money for other necessities)
- Can go to trade-related shows and meet industry leaders when promoting your company
- Can get wholesale or discounted prices on many products
- True freedom, and you get to see benefits of your hard work
- All personal-growth programs and business training and trips are tax deductible

The Bad and the Horrendous

- Setting your own hours can mean you're always on the job
- Income fluctuations with the business
- Income depends on *you* creating work or finding markets
- Takes time for a start-up company to build a customer base
- You are responsible for everything it takes to run your company: bookkeeping, advertising, customer service, taxes, cleaning—*everything*
- No sick pay, holiday pay, or unemployment benefits
- Have to make sure you don't overextend your or the company's finances
- Requires discipline regarding necessary business expenses—writing off too many expenses can create debt quickly
- You are responsible for bills even if company income takes a hit
- Can vacation yourself into debt
- Without business training or mentors, you can make bad business decisions
- You are responsible for the product or service you provide

Many people don't choose one or the other. You can have a regular job and also run a small business on the side. Some on-the-side businesses grow to the point that their owners are ready to walk away from their day job and step into the business full-time.

Either way, whether working a job or self-employed, I still follow the Freedom Jar system. My kids have been running their bunny business, dividing their money into the various categories, and have saved up enough to start a retail division of their business without any debt at all. The long-term savings part of their business money bought them bunny cages, brushes, and treats for bunnies. Now when they have someone pick up a bunny, often they have the cage and accessories for them as well. Now a forty-dollar sale is often worth over a hundred fifty. There is much you can do to reduce or eliminate the risks of self-employment. It just takes a little planning.

For me, the decision was easy, I love being my own boss. Yes, there have been many challenges, but I can grow and build with each one and really create the life of my dreams, on my terms.

There is no right or wrong choice. Whether you want to work for someone else or have your own company is up to you. Take a look at the pros and cons of both and see what makes you happier. And have your child do the same.

Chapter 7

Discovering the Right Business Idea

Sooner or later, most kids are going to want to make additional money. There are several options. You can add new chores to their list for extra cash. Or perhaps it's time to talk about *getting into business.*

The opportunities for business are hiding in plain sight—in the problems, challenges, or needs of the people you want to do business with. For example, if your kid loves dogs, ask them, "What kinds of problems might a dog owner have?"

These are just a few examples:

- Busy pet owners may not have enough time, which makes walking the dog every day (let alone twice a day) a problem. But a lack of time for the owner spells "OPPORTUNITY" for your child.

- And if there's too little time to walk the dog, there's likely no time to clean up the yard. So—bingo!—an entrepreneurial niche for the young neighborhood poop-scooping specialist.

- Perhaps they're going away and need a pet sitter for a few days, but they don't want to leave their dog in a kennel.

When you're deciding on a new business, it's important to find something that handles a problem for your customer by allowing you to provide the perfect solution for them. If you make the solution simple and affordable, it will be easy to sell. You may even decide to offer a free trial or half-price special for first-time customers, to let them see how good you are at little or no risk to them. We'll discuss marketing ideas in depth in a later chapter. There are many low-cost or even free ways to promote your great ideas.

The next thing to consider is the start-up cost. Ideally, you want the initial outlay as low as possible. As your child's business grows and their enthusiasm for it grows, they can reinvest in their business, upgrade, or purchase new equipment. See chapter 9, "Getting Started with a Small Business."

My favorite cost for business start-up is ZERO dollars. My second favorite is under fifty dollars. The following list gives fifty business ideas that your child can start for under fifty dollars. Some of the ideas that require equipment, such as a camera or a computer, are assuming that your child already has a camera or computer of their own, or has access to these.

The best way for you to use this list is as a platform to discuss ideas. Let your child's creativity go wild. This is not the time to put the brakes on their creative talents. Talk to them about what's happening in your neighborhood, what needs they see, and how they can help. Parents, write the ideas down as they come, and encourage your kids to continue their own list, inspired by these ideas. Also, chapter 12 has inspiring stories of what other kids have done. At this stage, it's important not to say anything negative about the ideas. Even the craziest idea can be an amazing success. If Steve Jobs had listened to all the naysayers, we would not have had iPod, iPad, or iPhone. If Alexander Graham Bell had allowed his critics to dissuade him, we wouldn't have the telephone. Let your kids dream big; then work with them to find a manageable starting place that resonates with them.

1. Lemonade stand
2. Gardening / yard care
3. Dog walking
4. Babysitting
5. Mowing lawns
6. Pet sitting / dog washing & grooming
7. Housecleaning / office cleaning
8. Garage cleaning & organizing
9. Stable cleaning
10. Horse exercising
11. Baking
12. Elderly care
13. Growing and selling Indian corn and fancy gourds for autumn decor
14. Tutoring
15. Writing, editing
16. Face painting
17. Snow shoveling
18. Summer camp jobs
19. Delivering papers
20. Flyer delivery

21. Meal preparation
22. Grocery shopping
23. Fence painting, garage painting
24. Interior painting
25. Rabbit breeding
26. Hamster breeding
27. DJ-ing
28. E-book creation
29. Neck warmers crafting & sales
30. Creating ads/fliers, graphic design
31. Photo editing
32. Photography: sports teams, portraits, pets, etc.
33. Pool cleaning
34. Car washing
35. Pottery making
36. Video editing
37. Computer troubleshooting, repairs
38. Bike repairs, fixing flats
39. Window cleaning
40. Search engine optimization
41. Facebook marketing
42. Web or graphic design
43. Sewing/alterations
44. Cake decorating
45. Event/party planning & decorating
46. Candle making
47. Woodworking
48. Jewelry making
49. Gourmet dog treats
50. Transcribing

Of course, your child's age and maturity will be a big factor in what they can venture into. Rules and guidelines need to be established to make sure that your child's safety is the first priority. Brainstorming sessions should be fun and playful. Make sure that everyone enjoys the process, or you've lost them before they begin.

The Right Business

My Favorite Things Exercise

1. Set a timer for five minutes.

2. For five minutes straight, brainstorm all the things your child loves to do. Write everything down, whether it's riding bikes, playing video games, ride horses, reading comic books, or chasing lizards. Forget about being practical! Keep your pen moving and the favorite things coming. Have fun with it! While they are writing (or while you are writing for them), ask the following questions to spark ideas:

   • What do you love to do?

   • How do you enjoy spending your free time?

   • What is your favorite thing to do?

   • What are some kind things that you had fun doing for people?

3. When the timer goes off—STOP. You're done.

4. Pick the top four items—the four things your kid most loves to do.

5. What are some problems or challenges that others have in this area? Example: if bike riding was one of the top four for your child, problems or challenges might include the need to replace a spoke or a chain, a flat tire, the need for lubrication or a brake adjustment, the need for an older riding partner or someone to teach bike safety.

6. Do this for each of the top four items. Then, for each item, take these challenges and write down solutions that you could get paid for providing. For example, you could lube and tune up bikes, fix flats, start a bike club, teach kids bike safety and road rules, teach technical skills.

7. Go through the list of problems and solutions and see if there's something there that you could see starting as a business. Think about who would be your customers and how much you would charge. (We'll go into more detail on determining what to charge in another chapter.)

8. Find out how many potential customers would be interested in what you have in mind. You can do this in a variety of ways. Ask your friends and neighbors. Put an online ad in the community newspaper or on something like Craigslist or Kijiji. If you see there is a demand, then it's time to start planning your new business.

Really listen to what they enjoy. If playing outside is on the list, then babysitting, gardening, or dog walking may be just the thing. Keep an open mind. If they don't have an answer to the questions, move on. Also, it's important that your kids not see this as the business they'll be doing for the rest of their life. (Although it could happen, it isn't all that likely.)

Your child may come up with a business idea "outside the box"—not from anything in the above exercise. You may be eating dinner one night and they may come up with a fantastic idea. Often, this exercise will not flush out their final choice but will plant a seed of what to think about and look for.

Think of this as an opportunity for your kids to try on what they like. If they decide on something, get started, and then realize it isn't what they were looking for—that it's just not a good fit—they can go back to the drawing board and try again. Changing is not the same thing as failing. Failing is falling down and not getting back up. Changing is recognizing that something is not a fit, and taking action to change it. Just one of the life lessons they will learn from this experience is how to deal with challenges, obstacles, and disappointments. Keeping a positive outlook throughout is itself a valuable lesson.

I have not failed. I've just found 10,000 ways that won't work.
—Thomas Edison

Getting Started with a Small Business

First things first: has your child picked a business to start? If not, go back to chapter 8, "Discovering the Right Business Idea."

Picking a Name and URL

Your child's new business will need a name. Try to get something catchy and memorable—something fun. Be careful not to make it too long, hard to pronounce, or hard to remember. My daughters breed and sell rabbits. Their business name is *Bunnyville*. I give riding lessons at *Five Star Ranch*. So have fun with it, and don't try to comb all the nine universes for the one perfect name.

Brainstorm a list of names. Be silly; be serious; play on words. Once you've done this, look over the list and see if any of them really pop out at you. Pick the best five names on the list. Then check online and see what URLs or domain names are available. It's usually around ten dollars a year to get and keep a URL, and with so much of today's business happening online, it's probably a worthwhile investment. If your child's business does not need an Internet presence, then you can skip the URL. I would really think about it, though. It's not much money, and if the business expands and they keep it for some time, they may find that they will use it later. Or it may make the business more valuable if the time comes to sell it. So if you get the URL right away, then it's reserved and available should you ever decide to create a Web site. And while we're on the subject, there are lots of places that have free and easy Web site set-up. If you have a teen, they can most likely do it themselves.

Next, go out and talk to people you know. Let them know your child is starting a business, and ask for feedback on the names. My daughters did a survey to see which name would get the most votes. So take your top five and start asking around. They can ask the server at the restaurant, friends and family, their schoolteacher, the person helping you in the shoe store, and so on. It's a good idea to get input from a wide variety of people. This will also get your child talking about their business and possibly drumming up some interest, as well as making it feel real for your child and building the excitement and momentum.

Exercise: List all your ideas for your child's new business name, and then circle the five best names.

_____

_____

_____

_____

_____

_____

_____

Equipment and Supplies

The next thing is to figure out all the supplies they'll need to get started.

- For a gardening business, they will need gardening tools, gloves, and proper shoes.
- A photography business will require a camera, computer, and editing software.
- A lemonade stand will need a table, cups, spoons, pouring jugs, lemonade mix, and ice.

You get the idea. Ideally, they'll start out with things they already have and can use, rather than spending a lot of money before they've made any. Explain that the start-up cost is a business expense, but the lower the expenses, the bigger—and sooner—the profits. It's a great time to start learning about managing costs.

If they do need some equipment and supplies, maybe they can find secondhand items that cost less than new ones. You can look online and in the paper, and ask friends and neighbors if they have the items you need for sale or trade. (Perhaps your child can even do some cleaning or chores for the items instead of paying cash. The barter system can work even as the business expands.) Also, garage sales can be a great place to shop for what they need.

If they ultimately do need to spend money on supplies, you can lend it to them. Create a contract, in which they agree to pay the amount back in whatever terms are fair for the situation. I would charge no interest or perhaps a very small amount, but you could talk about how it would work if the bank were lending them money, so they start to understand the concept. The contract is really about understanding and committing to the terms that they have agreed to—making it official. If you decide to give them the start-up costs, that's fine, too, but if you do, don't come back later, when they're making money, and ask for repayment then. Be clear from the beginning what the terms are. This, too, is an important teaching for them to learn.

Appendix F has a chart for listing supplies, where to get them, what the cost will be, and whether those items are owned by the new entrepreneur or are on loan. If your child is borrowing anything, make sure they understand that they alone are responsible for its care.

Pricing the Product or Service

This is an interesting area. It really comes down to two approaches: charge a low price so that you have more sales, or charge more and give your product or service an air of exclusivity. The most important part is to determine what it will cost your child to make the product they are selling, or how long it will take them to provide the service. Then they just have to decide how much their time is worth. It's also important that kids see that they have value and can charge for it. If it's going to take them longer than an experienced person, let's say, to patch a bike inner tube, then they could charge for the job, not by the hour. Much of the pricing will be determined by what other local people charge for the same service, and what people are willing to pay—that is, what the market will bear.

A great starting place, once the price is determined, is to have an "opening special," to let people try out what your child is selling. Maybe a half-price tune-up for the first bike, or one free lawn mowing when you sign up for a month of weekly mowings, or a free sample of lemonade (could have mini cups to give away in hopes of selling a full glass), or a free bonus for the first ten customers.

Exercise: What is the price that others charge for the same or a similar product or service? If there is no exact comparison, find the next closest thing.

_____

_____

Exercise: How is your child going to price the product or service? Brainstorm several different ways to package it, and the price they will charge.

_____

_____

_____

_____

Money Management

Just as your personal money is divided into categories to ensure balance and growth in your personal life, so should the business money be. Below are the percentages that Ashley and Caitlyn use in their bunny business. This is just an example. Take a look and see if it works—if not, adjust it to fit your kids' situation. Right now the girls are looking at adjusting their percentages because they are accumulating too much money in areas of their business that they are not using, so they want to reallocate and possibly give themselves a bigger paycheck now that they have a stable financial footing and a good cushion to handle unexpected expenses.

- Necessities: 40%
- Learn: 10%
- Plan: 15%
- Paycheck: 30%
- Angel: 5%

Once the money is divided the girls take their paycheck and divide it into their personal jars. Again, do what works for you and your kids. Be prepared to adjust if needed. There is no right or wrong answer.

Final Details

Once they've established the price and are in the process of gathering equipment and supplies, here are a few more things to look at:

- Does your child need business cards? There are many low-cost ways to do this on your own computer, or maybe your local printer is running a card special. You may even have your child explain to the printer what they are doing, and see if they can maybe get sponsored or given a discount.
- What about flyers to advertise their product or service? This can be a flyer handcrafted by your child, or they can help designing it on the computer. Include how to get in touch with the business (phone and e-mail, for example), the name of the business, what the business will do for the potential customer, and possibly a special opening offer.
- Logo. A picture or symbol that will represent the business is a fun step that you can add at any time.

Advertising

Now that your kids are ready, they need to let people know what they're doing. Maybe there's already a bit of a buzz going around because they've been talking to people about what they are setting up. Now it's time to find customers. So how do you find them (and find them inexpensively)? Do you know who your target audience is? Your child needs to be thinking about who will purchase their product or service. Is it a neighborhood business, such as lawn mowing, driveway shoveling, or car washing? Or is it something with a little wider local market area, such as babysitting, baking, or rabbit breeding? Or is it something national or international in scope, such as a variety of online business, e-books, or photo editing?

By "target audience," I mean who, specifically, will be your child's customers? For instance, if they're doing face painting, it will probably be kids from two to twelve years old. If their operation is

Time to Advertise

under the maple tree in the front yard, it will be kids within walking distance of the house.

Alec has a fantastic creative idea that's all about pipe cleaners. He has discovered how to make everything from airplanes with pilots and weapons, to dragons with flames shooting out of their mouths, to motorcycles with riders and even a sidecar! He is taking this creative idea and photographing his progress for each design. He plans to make simple how-to videos and post on YouTube to develop interest in what he's doing. The next stage will include selling his designs as online links, and possibly an e-book. This is a great example of creativity at work. His target market will be creative kids from 9 to 14 years old.

Exercise: What is the chosen business?

_____

Who is the target audience? What is the typical customer's age and gender? Where do they live? Where do they socialize? What do they read? List anything you can think of that will help you home in on where to find the right customers.

_____
_____
_____
_____
_____
_____

Advertising and marketing is a part of business that is very exciting for me because there are so many low- or no-cost ways of doing things. There are many ways to promote your child's business. If it's a lemonade stand or a yard sale, posters at intersections leading to your home could work. Put a small ad in the local paper, or maybe the school would allow you to put something in the announcements or add something to its newsletter or Web site. You could see if you can set up a lemonade stand at the park, especially if there are sports games happening there.

If your child will be donating a percentage to a charity (which is recommended in the jar system of dividing your money), you may be able to get media coverage. Let the local papers and radio stations know that your child is starting a business doing xyz and is giving 5 percent or 10 percent to a local charity, and would they like to do an interview or cover the story? And if your kids are old enough, let *them* do the talking. All flyers need to state that X percentage of profits will be going to charity Y.

Social media is huge right now. It is also free. If you have teens, they can tell you all about it. Or this may need a parent's help. See about doing a Facebook fan page that will be filtered by parents. And as the parent, investigate other social media platforms.

Social media is one of the fastest growing free ways to connect with people and share your message. Facebook, Twitter, YouTube, and a multitude of other platforms are available. If you aren't sure how to navigate these sites, then hire a local high school kid to come and show you and your child how to do it. Or you can look at YouTube and look up a "how to" for the area you want to learn.

You may be heartened to know that when I started all this I was completely clueless about all the computer stuff that I do so effortlessly now. It just takes some time and fiddling.

One of the key things to have is a fan page. Then you can spread the word about what's happening, and create events such as a grand opening, opening-day special, or Mother's Day discount. Have fun and be creative. You can share great information about the benefits of your product or service through articles or videos that other people have written.

A YouTube channel can be great if you're trying to promote a video, such as a how-to. The videos need not be fancy or seamlessly edited. If you have the skills, fine, go for it, but it isn't necessary. Most cell phones can take videos, and many can upload straight to YouTube. It could even be a video on the benefits of a well cared-for lawn, which you found on YouTube and added to your like list. My daughters sell bunnies, and they are looking to start a series of bunny facts on YouTube, to show people helpful skills, such as how to clip their bunny's nails or how to litter-train their bunny. Once they do this they will gear this toward the book they are creating on how to care for bunnies. It has taken them seven years in their business to get to this point, so there's no terrible rush. Don't try to make all the great ideas happen at once. Start with the basic concept, and add steps as they present themselves and as your child is ready to tackle them.

Some additional sites that I am not as familiar with are LinkedIn, MySpace, Digg, StumbleUpon, MyBlogLog, Reddit, Flickr, Blogster, SocialVibe, and many more.

A blog site can be extremely popular and helpful. It's also a great way for your child to get motiovated to write a short article once a week.

It's a great idea to have a Web site. They're easy to set up at a very low cost. Many offer free programs and hosting.

I started a podcast that I post weekly to promote my book. I include interviews and information on timely events, and people and information all to do with creating Money Smart Kids. If your child has a lawn-mowing service, they could do customer interviews, fun facts about lawn care, and more. The idea is to build interest and create a relationship with the reader or listener. The basic format is free, and you can add bells and whistles as needed, at a minimal cost.

E-mail campaigns are another great way to promote your kid's business. You can start to develop a list through other online ads or through getting signed up for a special offer. Perhaps they can get the local church to send a flyer to its e-mail list. Think about what can be done as a benefit to the person or company that sends the flyer out to their list. Perhaps a free service or product by your child, or maybe they can do some chores for the person in exchange for the publicity.

For a neighborhood business, door-to-door is great (parent supervised and age appropriate, of course). Also, flyers can be sent through the post office at minimal cost. Press releases can go to local community centers, and they can post flyers on community boards. There are lots of places, such as Kijiji or Craigslist, where you can get free listings online.

You can set up a fund-raiser to raise money for a cause that you believe in and raise awareness of your business. Talking to the local news stations and newspapers to offer an interview with a budding young entrepreneur is always a great idea. Papers love feel-good stories that support the community and its members.

Kids can also go through the family phone list and let friends and family know what they are doing. They may get some business or some possible contacts who may be interested in their product or service.

Write an article, and have it listed in the local community paper or on the community Web site. Don't make it *too* promotional. Make sure you are adding value to the reader.

Find local clubs or associations that relate to your child's business. Often you can advertise for free in their newsletters. You can create a press release and send it to local papers and associations that may have people who are interested. It really will depend on what the service or product is and how busy your child or you want to be. If your child wants to do lawn care, it may be that making some flyers and going door to door in your neighborhood is enough to generate all the business they can handle. So you don't have to follow *all* the above suggestions. Simply take time with your child to find out how many customers they want to start with (or have time for), and decide on the best way to get that many customers.

Exercise: How many customers does your child want to have each week?_____ How much time will this take?_____ How many customers do they want to have six months from now?_____

How many units does your child want to sell each week?_____ Each month?_____ In a year?_____

As with every other step in the business, your child needs to be totally involved here. Their age and aptitude will determine how much guidance you give them. If they are in their teens, they can come up with some creative ideas on their own and bounce them off you. If they're younger, then you can have a brainstorming session with them. Instead of telling them all your ideas, try asking them leading questions that will help them come up with the ideas themselves, and then add some new ones to the list.

Once you have a list of ideas, pick the top two or three that fit your situation best, and get started. Pick an opening day or a time frame for everything to begin, and get ready for business.

Exercise: List the top marketing/advertising ideas that apply to your child's business. Circle the top one to three ideas that your child will focus on first.

_____

_____

_____

_____

_____

_____

_____

When I opened my horseback riding business at 16 years old I created an opening weekend special. Trail rides would be eight dollars an hour instead of ten. I posted flyers everywhere. The film *City Slickers* was in the theaters, so I would go every evening when the movie was showing, and put a flyer on every car. Yes, it was time consuming and maybe even a little irritating to the drivers of those cars. But I was determined to have a full day. I had a few reservations and was very excited. Opening day came, the horses were ready, and the place looked great. I waited and waited. My first group that reserved didn't show up. As the day went on I got very sad, and at four p.m. my mom and my boyfriend at the time came out with eight dollars each. I took them on a great trail ride and made a whopping sixteen dollars on my first day of business.

I tell you that story not to depress or discourage you, but to acknowledge that it takes time to get things moving. It also takes a bit of experimenting to figure out how to reach your target audience. So if your child's opening day is quieter than expected, just keep going. Within a few weeks I was filling my weekends, and in a very short time I was making a thousand dollars a day.

Every business goes through ups and downs. Simply look at why a slump may be happening, and what action needs to happen to correct it. In fact, this is a great way to look not just at business but at life in general. This is another set of life lessons that your child will learn by being in business: how to evaluate and adapt.

Check appendix G, "Resources," for Web sites that can help you create videos; do testimonials; and create digital, DVD, or audio products for a fraction of the regular cost. One such site is called Fiverr.com. This is one of my favorites, and I have many things done here, including a mock-up book cover professionally done for just five bucks. You'll find more information on the "Resources" page. Actually, Fiverr is a great place for you and your child to look for business ideas. Maybe there is something that your child could sell at that site.

It all boils down to this: how big does your child want to grow the business? If it's an e-book on how to care for your new kitten, you can set up to take unlimited orders with little or no human intervention, once it is set up. But if your child is going to mow lawns in the neighborhood, then three yards per week may be all that fits in between school and other activities.

Take a look at all the above ideas, and start with one or two that fit your child's ability and business of choice. From there, they can then play around with other ideas.

Chapter 9

Growing Up
What Your Kids Need to Know
before They Are on Their Own

Okay, so your kids know how to manage money. They've even learned how to run a small business, all under your watchful, loving guidance. One day they will be on their own, juggling rent, food, car payments, and more. This chapter covers all the things they will need to know about money when they are over 18, such as how credit cards work, how to manage using credit cards, how to build credit, what they should have in order *before* they get their first place on their own, and much more.

Too many young adults head out to college or university totally unprepared for the shift. The average debt for a student leaving college is over twenty-three thousand dollars. Many have already maxed out the credit cards they got when the promoters came to the schools during orientation.

We'll cover mortgages and other large purchases, such as cars, to give a full overview of what lies ahead. The more *we* look forward with some positive ideas on how to handle these challenges, the higher *their* chances of success will be.

There is no good reason to wait until they're 18 to talk about financial responsibility. Money is a topic that needs to be part of the regular conversation. Starting early with all this information will give them a healthy base, and confidence in making the best decisions for their financial future.

When your child begins to think about and get ready for this transition (if not before), the "Necessities" jar needs to be added to the other categories. This way, they have more time to

Graduation Shock

get used to the change in spending habits, and can start to save up for this expense. Refer back to the chapter on teaching your kids to handle money.

Postsecondary Education

If your child is planning on attending college, university, or some type of vocational schooling after high school, there are several things you need to talk about together. (If they're still in grade school, this conversation can wait.)

- Will you be helping support your child's postsecondary education?
- How much are you both willing and able to contribute?
- How much does your child have saved up in the education jar?
- What scholarships, bursaries, and grants are available to help fund your child's education? (They need to research this area, but you may need to lend a hand.)
- What is the overall cost of the program, including tuition, fees, books, living accommodation, transportation, food, and entertainment?
- Does the average wage of the profession or career that they are studying justify the education expense?
- Who are the potential employers they would like to work with after schooling?
- Can they live at home while going to school, and for a period of time afterward?
- What can be done to minimize the level of debt at the time of their graduation?

Getting a Job

- Any small-business skills and experience can help make a great impact on your resumé.

- In putting together a resumé, make sure that your child includes how they can benefit the company (saving time and money, making a system more efficient, and how their small-business skills make them conscious of the "behind the scenes" parts of running a business.

- Remind them to gear their resumé to the *specific* company they are applying to. No one likes to get a generic boilerplate that goes to everyone.

- When looking at a job, also evaluate whether it is right for your child. (They will need to be fully involved in this.) Are there benefits? Does it work with the school schedule? Is the pay scale appropriate?

- They may choose to continue with a part-time small business while in school (such as tutoring, mowing lawns, shoveling sidewalks, or babysitting) to earn some spending money.

A Place of Their Own

- This is where the long-term savings account comes into play. How much do they have saved up to get an apartment? I would suggest having at least five months' rent (and utilities)—first and last month's rent plus three months—saved up before they make the leap. This will give them a cushion if they should get laid off or experience some other change in circumstances.

- What does the place include, and what are the extras? Will there be water, gas and electric, Internet and cable access, and phone bills on top of the rent? Determine how much each will cost, and see how you can cut costs. Maybe they can skip cable—after all, studies and work are going to take up a good chunk of their time, anyway. Or maybe they can get a roommate to share expenses.

- It's a great idea to start saving a year or more ahead of time, so they don't have to dig themselves into a financial hole to start living in their own place.

- What about furnishing the space? Is there an old sofa in the den, or a dinette that's on its way out the door? Also, garage sales are a great way to fill any furniture gaps. There are many places to get furniture on the cheap. A word to the wise: Avoid falling into the easy trap of getting all brand-new furniture on the "don't pay for a year" plan. That year will roll by, and they may be stuck paying for a houseful of year-old furniture just about the time they are ready to move. They can sleep just as soundly on second-hand furniture and add new pieces as they save for them.

- Dishes and everyday household necessities. This may be a good chance to clear out some of the stuff you never use anymore that's just cluttering up the basement. I have seen Facebook posts by people who were getting a place and would love to help recycle extra household items. Many of your friends and relatives likely have stuff sitting in their cupboards that your kids need and that they may never use. Ask them—people love to recycle stuff, especially if it's going to someone they know.

- When looking at places, along with cost, consider location (proximity to work and school, as well as a safe neighborhood). There are apartments, shared houses, basement apartments, and many more options.

- Consider proximity to public transit (make sure this is in the budget, too), or parking if they have a vehicle.
- Is there potential for a rent-to-own situation? Don't be afraid to think big! Depending on how it's structured, this could be an amazing way to have a place and still be working toward ownership.

Credit Cards

- The most important thing for your child to understand here is that credit cards are *not* "free money." In fact, used irresponsibly, they are about the most expensive money around. They usually have a very high interest rate, so they should *never* hold a balance from month to month. It's a simple concept: pay the credit card *in full* each month to avoid paying massive amounts in interest.
- Credit card companies make most of their money from people who carry an ongoing balance on their cards.
- Interest rates can be 25 percent or more. This is simply throwing your hard-earned money away.
- Use credit cards with points on them. If you're going to be spending on them anyway, you can earn free rewards. (Be mindful of annual fees.)
- If you simply pay the minimum balance on your cards, there is a good chance that they will never be clear of that debt, and that the items you bought way back when could end up costing you double the original price, or even more!

Establishing Good Credit

- One really good reason for having a credit card is to help establish credit for when your child wants to buy a home or a car.

- It's essential that any loans or credit cards be paid on time, since any late payments are tracked by your credit score. This score is something that lenders check. So will the landlord when your child is applying for an apartment.
- A lower credit score means higher interest rates on loans or credit cards.

Buying a Vehicle

- A vehicle is an asset, but one of the lowest-performing ones. Not only do cars not go up in value, they need maintenance and additional money put into them as they get older—money that you generally don't get back.
- A new vehicle drops in value (as much as 10 percent) the second it pulls off the dealer's lot.
- A car is generally the second biggest expense after rent or mortgage.
- When looking at car options, also think about (and research) the amount of insurance that the car will require. A sports car will be much higher than a minivan, for example.
- A great idea is to budget in your jar system the amount you would like to spend monthly on a car, and save it for at least six months. This will give your child the chance to see whether that amount is feasible on their income, and it will help them accumulate the money for the down payment (or maybe the whole price, if the car is used). Starting early on this can mean a significant savings in their monthly expenses later.
- Take an expert with you to look at used vehicles, and you should always get a qualified mechanic to check it before

you buy, to make sure it won't need major repairs in the short term.

- Have at least three months' worth of payments saved to cover the possibility of losing or changing jobs.

Buying a House

- It may seem way too early to think about this, but even just having conversations about it will plant seeds for your child. If they can have a basic understanding about the cost of a home now, they will be more prepared when the time comes.
- Have a plan or goal for when they want to become a home owner, and then work backward to see how much they need to save each month or year for a good down payment.
- Look at the options and incentives for first-time home owners. If they have planned well enough, some kids can make their first move out of the family home and into a home of their own, with monthly payments comparable to what their friends may be paying as rent.
- Consider a home with a spare room or a finished (or finishable) basement they can rent out to supplement the mortgage payment.
- Don't forget closing costs and move-in costs. Refer to the "A Place of Their Own" section above for everything they'll need to furnish the home. And remember, you don't have to buy the top of the line at first—get furnishings that "will do," and you can always trade up later.
- Location is even more important when buying a home than when renting, since it will help determine value down the road.

Insurance

- There is a whole smorgasbord of insurance available out there—everything from product insurance to replace your computer or fridge to life, disability, and more.

- Some insurance is optional, and some insurance is mandatory.

- Car insurance, for example, is the law. You must insure your car. The type and amount of insurance you can determine with a little research and the advice of a professional in the industry.

- When banks lend you money for your house the fire insurance is usually included in your payment. Ask your banker for more information on this type of insurance.

- Disability insurance will help you if something happens to you making you unable to work. Some employers offer this as part of their benefit plan. If not, it can be purchased separately.

- Like disability insurance, life insurance is not as critical when your child is single, but becomes much more important when a spouse and children enter the picture.

- Health insurance in Canada generally covers expenses over and above what the health care system covers (for example, prescriptions, dental). In the United States, health insurance is an absolute necessity. Again, some employers will cover this or a portion of it. It's a good idea to determine what is included, and then see if you need to supplement it with additional insurance.

- I offer a few tips that I've found to be helpful, but you need to talk to a professional in this area.

Well, the above list may seem a bit daunting. Not all the expenses are necessary, but it's a great idea to start these discussions now. Most kids have no idea what it costs to live an adult life, and knowing this information can help them become that much more conscious of their spending habits right now. The whole idea of looking ahead is to be able to set themselves up for success by *planning* for these expenses, rather than scrambling to make ends meet when they have not factored in certain things. This list is by no means complete. Many areas, cultures, and people have additional needs and expenses and may need to prepare for different future expenses. The key is to raise your child's awareness of the kinds of things they need to think about.

Chapter 10

My Beginnings as an Entrepreneur

When I was 7 years old I had my first lemonade stand. I spent the day mixing and pouring drinks for anyone who came by. At the end of the day, I had a pocketful of change (and even some folding money!) and the pride of doing something to make other people happy. I don't remember all the details of the day, but I do remember how excited I was to buy something I wanted with real money that I had earned.

When I was 12 years old I started another business venture: I decided to make crafts and sell them. For weeks, I worked on knitting Barbie purses and making Barbie chairs out of clothespins. This venture was not nearly as successful as my first one, because my marketing and location were totally wrong. I lived on a highway and parked myself in the front yard with a small sign, hoping someone would stop and take a look. I waited the whole day, and not one person stopped. That would have been a good time to fold everything up and quit, but I didn't. I found other places where I could sell or give away the crafts I had made. This ended up being a great learning experience in how *not* to do things—every bit as important as learning what *to* do!

Blondie's Story

Like many young girls, all I ever wanted was a horse of my own. I didn't think this would ever happen. When I was 11, I volunteered at the local trail-riding stable. That's where I met Blondie. She was a beautiful palomino pony (but I called her a horse). I fell in love. Every time I was there Blondie got lots of extra attention from me. I did my best to ride her every time we took customers out on trails. Each night, I came home and talked my family's ears off about my day and, especially, my Blondie. My parents must have been listening, because on my twelfth birthday we drove out to the farm, where I learned that she was my birthday present. I cried tears of joy. For many years, Blondie and I spent countless hours at the barn (we built one at home) and on the trails. She was my best friend, my protector, and the best counselor I've ever had. Every year on her birthday (the anniversary of the day I got her), we would go on a trail ride. We would go bareback, and when we got to one of my favorite spots I would get off Blondie and take off her bridle, and she would follow me. Sometimes we would meet someone walking their dog (on a leash), but Blondie was totally free. I would often run off in front of her, and she would break into a trot to catch up. When we got to my second favorite spot in the woods I would sit down and read a book, and Blondie would munch away on the grass, coming over and nuzzling me for an occasional treat. When we were ready we would get riding again and head home. We were an amazing team. It was my experience with Blondie while volunteering at the stable that started me thinking about my own trail-riding stable. When Blondie surprised us by getting pregnant (bonus two for one!) I was on the way to having my own string of trail horses. So now I just needed four more horses and equipment to get started.

When I was 15 I decided that I actually wanted to start a horseback-riding facility. We had two horses at the time, and I thought that would be a great start to a trail-riding business. So I went to the student ventures program and started my business plan.

Blondie and Gail

I thought about how many horses I was going to need, how many saddles, and how much all that was going to cost. Then I estimated what I was going to earn, and put many hours into the proposal. When it was time to go to student ventures for the summer business loan, I decided to test it out on my parents first. After my whole presentation about my new business, my parents looked at me and said, "Okay, we'll do it." I was confused. I didn't know what they were talking about—they had decided to lend me the money to start my business! I remember being so excited and thankful for this opportunity. Then fear crept in—those little monsters that slink around in your head and tell you that you can't do it and what were you thinking, anyway! Thankfully, I didn't listen.

I enlisted the help of some of my horse friends to help me find horses that would be suitable for my trail-riding business. I was lucky enough to find out about a farm that was closing down. So I called the owner up and took my friends and family for a trail ride. I let them know that I was planning on starting a trail-riding enterprise and I wanted their best trail horses. When we got there I stood back and watched all my friends and family getting on these trail horses, paying close attention to each horse's behavior and the rider's reactions. For that hour, I stayed at the back of the line and watched even more. When the time came for the auction of the trail horses I had my list ready and knew which ones I wanted to bring home with me. Luckily, I was able to bring home two of the three horses that I really wanted. The third horse, I ended up getting about a week later. Then I found another wonderful horse on a quiet farm. Now I had the six horses that I needed to begin my business.

I created a logo and advertisements and started spreading the word. As June 15, 1986, drew closer the opening day of my new business was about to become a reality. I went to community boards, posted in grocery stores, set up a booth in the mall, and even went to theaters where *City Slickers* was playing to get exposure for the grand opening. My opening-day special was $8 a trail (now $40), and I already had a few reservations for riders. Then I waited . . . and waited. No one showed up. As I told you earlier, at four p.m. my mom and boyfriend came out with sixteen dollars, and I took them on a great trail ride. As the summer progressed my days filled, and by the end of the summer I was earning up to a thousand dollars a day. Not bad for a 16-year-old girl!

During the winter, I would work a retail job, since there was very little income from the horses. After graduating from high school, I went to Humber College in Toronto for their equine program. I became a certified coach and began teaching lessons.

As the business grew and my parents saw that I had found my calling, we looked at building a barn. My income wouldn't support the loan. So my parents built the barn and we started accepting boarders. That end of the business was my parents'. So now I had a business partner. Several years later, I was able to secure a loan for an indoor arena, which turned my seasonal business into a year-round facility where we offered lessons all winter long. It also kept us out of the rain and extreme sun in the other seasons. First it was just trail rides, then lessons, then summer camp, clinics. Five Star Ranch continued to expand. There was even an eight-month full-time coaching program to prepare riders to become riding coaches.

After attending Humber College and attaining my Equine Canada Level 1 Western Coaching Certificate, I went on to Seneca College for the farrier program. Next I was off to Colorado for the . John Lyons Certification. I then continued my training in Equine Canada for the Level 2 Western Coaching Program Certification. And then off to Colorado once more for eleven weeks, stretched out over a year, to continue in my training education with John Lyons.

(John is a world-renowned horse trainer known as "America's most trusted horseman.") In 2008, I completed the accreditation program specializing in reining training with Josh Lyons (John's son).

Between the equine programs that I have taken, I have also attended many business and self-development programs. Continuing education has not only been an amazing experience, meeting super people and creating many magical memories, but it has been essential in the growth of my business.

Having my own business has enabled me to travel the world, be at home to raise my kids, and take advantage of opportunities I would never have had in a traditional job. Though the hours at the time seemed endless, I would not give it up for anything.

To conclude my story about Blondie, she was with me until just a few years ago. She went to the big pasture in the sky, leaving me with over twenty years of incredible memories. It is amazing what one little horse can do for a little girl, how much one decision can change your life. The cool thing is that you never know which decision is going to make this kind of impact—it's always a surprise. I'm sure my parents didn't know that getting this fat little pony for an excited girl turning 12 would set her up for a career that has spanned over twenty-six years now and counting. So don't underestimate the power of the decisions and choices you make, both for yourself and for your kids. Years later, you may look back and see how powerful the choices you made have been.

Chapter 11

Amazing Kids'
Stories and Interviews

Gail, it's a lemonade story . . . Our son Oliver wanted to earn some extra money to fill his X-Box bag to fund his share of the purchase with his brother. His mother and I would pay the other half.

We suggested setting up a lemonade stand on the nearby corner. It involved cups, lemonade, a cooler, ice, etc. Of course, the cost of these items didn't factor in, but that's to be expected for a 6-year-old. He did make a sign to advertise the cool beverage on a hot September day. It was the best use of the colored markers we'd seen in a long time.

Off we go to pitch his new business venture to any passerby who came along. I'm not sure what we enjoyed more—the looks on everyone's face as they drove by, amazed at anyone so young setting up a lemonade stand in today's age, as they recalled their own youth (straight out of the movie *Ratatouille*), or Oliver's comment that was soon to follow.

As the customers poured in giving Oliver a dollar or more for the 25-cent beverage and chatting as he poured each cup with a newfound passion, when we had a lull in the traffic we prompted him to get out there and hold up and wave his sign because he was the boss. To which he replied, "If I'm the boss, why do I have to wave the sign?"

He's a keeper.

—**Tom Leblanc**, Sudbury, Massachusetts

Gail, when my son was in air cadets and away at camp, and again when he was in college, he would supplement his income by purchasing large pizzas and then selling them off by the slice. He also wasn't afraid of doing someone's laundry for them or cooking them meals when they didn't know how to cook their own! He was very resourceful and made lots of spending money that way. I was very proud of him. He now works at a low-paying job but has saved some money with careful budgeting. He has made a good life for himself, his wife, and his unborn baby boy!

—**Kelly Reading Doherty**, Princeton, Ontario

Hi, Gail. Just a quick note to say that I am a single mom and everything we have, we own. I don't have any debt (until I buy a house). In order for Ali and me to be able to show on the quarter horse circuit, I needed to supplement my income (which is already decent) in order to justify spending that kind of money. My son has other expensive hobbies and is just a plain great kid, which is why he helps me with my business (I make horse tail extensions for show horses). I have two amazing children, and considering what we have been through, I am very proud of all three of us. I believe that the business makes us a stronger family. My children have always been a part of my business. Chandler is right there helping me make the product, and Ali is my marketing guru. She tells everyone about my product. They both also get dollars for every tail sold. Ali saves her money, and Chandler spends his. But they are both learning that money doesn't come from the mommy money tree and that I need to work for it and that if they want everything that we have, they need to help. It's a good lesson and will be helpful when they apply for a job. That is why Ali and I wanted to volunteer at your place. It is very good on their résumés. Great job on your book! You are an inspiration.

—**Elizabeth Gnoinski**, Brantford, Ontario

This is an Interview with Tom LeBlanc about his personal business experiences as a child:

Gail: I would really like to know what your experience is with creating an income or starting a small business, and how old you were when you did this.

Tom: A lot of this is a recollection of thoughts and memories that are sometimes fuzzy and other times burned in as if they happened yesterday.

My parents and two of my brothers ran a Sunday-only paper route, called the Joe, Tom, and Larry Sunday Paper, that encompassed Bradford and Haverhill, MA, over a period of four to five years. I started in the first grade, so at the age of 7.

We started at 4:00 in the morning, drove to the Fox Paper company in downtown Haverhill, to put the papers together. We would have to stuff the ad inserts into the papers and then load them into the car, a vintage station wagon with the classic wood-grain paneling. Everyone was there. It was a very busy place, even at that time of the morning. We got to know all the other guys who were delivering newspapers, just like we were.

Some memories I have are gassing up the car, since this was an endeavor that covered a lot of territory. I remember paying 17 cents a gallon for gasoline. I remember it vividly because my dad would always chime in with one of his classic catch-all phrases about the thieves and bandits who were ripping him off.

Coincidentally, I remember making 17 cents every time we ran to a door to drop a big heavy Sunday paper in between the storm door and the main door. I think I remember this because my mother did all the bookkeeping and she and I are really close. I probably overheard her telling someone else, because she would never tell me something like that.

I can remember sitting on the open tailgate of the station wagon and hopping off as I would grab four or five papers at once and hitting several houses as my father would drive up the street to meet us. It was hustle, hustle, hustle. My dad was a bit of a slave driver and wouldn't put up with any back talk.

We started small with 150 customers, and after buying several more routes, through "acquisition" we ended up with over 650 customers.

I'm not sure why we stopped. I'm sure we started because of the money—or lack of it, I should say. Money was tight, and this "cash" business was a way to enjoy skiing as a family: equipment, tickets, etc.

I remember vividly once a month dropping a small yellow envelope along with the paper, and picking up the envelopes with cash the next week. I remember even more vividly having to knock on the doors of the people who didn't pay us.

Gail: how did this shape who you are today?

Tom: I have always been self-sufficient—never needed to ask for help. There isn't very much that I can't do for myself.

I started officially working at the age of 14, with the use of a worker's permit that let me work two years early, and worked in a JOB ever since. The money that I saved was used to pay for my college education, two trips to Europe, to Austria and Chamonix [France] in high school with the ski club, and my first car.

Twenty years later I worked in Paris for two and a half years with my family and an engineering liaison with large medical companies like Siemens, Philips, and GE.

I started a software consulting company that ran for fourteen years. This was postcollege, and I used my love of mechanical engineering and computer science to generate productivity tools that automated the CAD/CAM design environment. I was selling parametric programming long before ether Solidworks or ProEngineer ever arrived on the scene. Unfortunately, I could never get my foot off the dock to do it full-time. I never had the training or mentor to help me facilitate that transition.

I am a reformed workaholic. I now enjoy many things and work smarter, not harder. Time is my most precious commodity.

Today, with the training from Peaks and CEO Space, the personal and business development is growing every day. I am starting a new business venture with my fiancée, launching a new brand called "There's a Towel for That." Our first product will be the Cat's Tongue Towel. A big piece of our mission is to give back to the community at large, specifically, donating 25 percent of our profits to the Dana-Farber Cancer Institute. For information, see our Web site, www.catsTongueTowels.com.

Gail: What skills and life lessons did you learn as a result of this experience?

Tom: Eventually I learned that my managers looked down on people who are too independent, always in the critical path. I have always felt that teamwork was a critical life skill. I like to say all of life's important lessons are learned on the kindergarten playground.

About Us

Bunnyville began in late 2004. That was when we (Ashley and Caitlyn) got our first bunny, Silver. She was a blue tort mini lop that Ashley got for her eighth birthday. Caitlyn (naturally) then wanted a bunny, too. Two weeks later, a fawn mini lop arrived for Caitlyn's sixth birthday. The people at the pet store had said they were both females. Well, they weren't, and five weeks later Bunnyville's first litter was born.

Ashley and Caitlyn did all the research they needed to take care of the babies, and quickly moved the father into a new cage. When the bunnies reached seven weeks they were sold to friends or to the pet store. This is how it went for a few years until Ashley and Caitlyn decided to expand their business.

In 2008, the two businessgirls began to look around for more bunnies. One by one, they found some pretty Holland lops and mini lops. While looking around, they fell in love with a new breed: lionheads. This expansion in bunnies also called for an expansion in cages and the cost of raising fourteen bunnies.

Ashley and Caitlyn created a fan page on Facebook and began selling on their own instead of to the pet stores. The bunnies have been taken to the Royal Winter Fair each year since 2009 and have won the best of breed in doe and litter, and multiple second places in standard and pet rabbit. Since 2004, Bunnyville has raised the quality of its lionheads and lops. Now we are selling pedigreed lionheads and are well on the way to pedigreed lops. In April 2012, Bunnyville's first shipment of cages and supplies came in. Now you can get everything you need for your bunny, right here!

That's our story so far. So Welcome to Bunnyville Rabbitry!

—Ashley and Caitlyn Haynes

I am really glad that I used the money-jar system for Bunnyville (the business my sister and I started). It really helps the business grow and be self-sufficient. I don't have to spend any of my own money on my business; it all comes from the money we receive from our customers. My sister and I have been running this business for about seven years, and we have no debt whatever! In fact, we're making money just by doing something that we love! It's a little tough sometimes cleaning all those cages, but it's well worth the time!

The money-jar system is really good because it also taught me how to be responsible with money. I split up all my income into different categories, and it helped me save more because I used to be a big spender. Now I can still spend money and save up for things, too. It seems as though I have more now that I use the different categories. For our business, my sister and I have also put the money system in place. One of the categories is for the absolute necessities of the business, such as rabbit food. Another one is for planning for larger things such as a new cage or rabbit, and then we have an educational account we can use to buy rabbit books or anything else that can help us learn more about rabbits and about other things that can help us out. We also have a charity account so that we can help out by donating money to people and animals that need it. The final category is our personal paycheck.

This is the money that my sister and I will then sort into our own accounts. I just think it's so cool that after all the expenses and sorting we are still making a good amount of money within and outside of our business!

—**Ashley Haynes**

Business:

Having a business was a great learning experience. There are many positive things I have learned. Though being in a business is a great learning experience and fun, make sure you can still be a kid. I highly suggest learning all about the world and how you can be successful—just make sure you have time for you. Create the structure for your life ahead, and this book will help you. If you are interested in starting a business, GO FOR IT! Be prepared, though, and know you will have to devote lots of time and face many challenges. Remember, never give up, and do what's right for *you*!

—**Caitlyn Haynes**

Jack's Story

When my 10-year-old son Jack started his own business, the first thing he did was look at the business options available to him. We discussed their viability as cash machines and analyzed their potential for cash flow. Right now you're probably thinking, "Lady, you wanted your kid to think about a *cash flow*? Isn't that a bit *much*?"

Nope, not at all. Cash flow is a critical piece to the success of any business. I wanted my son Jack to succeed—not for a day but for a lifetime. I knew that in teaching him to start his own business, I was also teaching him life skills. I had to abandon the notion that he was too young to understand things like cash flow and other business concepts. I was *not* teaching him how to *do a job*—I was teaching him how to *run a business*.

I wanted Jack to start a business in our neighborhood. This was important because of the personal contact and life skills he would learn through interacting with his neighbors. Internet businesses are great, but kids miss out on learning some key life skills, such as shaking hands, the important of eye contact, and basic sales techniques. To evaluate all the options open to Jack, we charted them:

We looked at all the criteria that were important to us, like not working on the weekends, steady income, and so on. The evaluation process made it easy for Jack to identify which service would be his cash machine and which services could provide ancillary streams of income.

His direction was clear, and in June he launched Jack's Garbage Valet and was transformed into a 10-year-old entrepreneur. Jack would offer to take his neighbors' garbage cans in and out each week for ten dollars a month.

While we worked on the tools he would need to build the business, like flyers and sales pitches, we studied the five basic business concepts he needed to learn:

- Marketing and Sales
- Accounting
- Execution
- Customer Service
- Follow-up

These concepts were easy to teach in the context of his garbage valet business, and I found that if I tied them back to something familiar, he caught on very quickly.

Teaching moments such as how to handle rejection, how to talk to an adult, the importance of eye contact, and how to properly execute a handshake came up every day we were out selling his business. As a result, he learned to have a thicker skin and be more assertive.

Having Jack start his business has been a huge success. As a result of starting his business, he has written a book and become a best–selling author!

Jack's book, *How to Let Your Parents Raise a Millionaire: A Kid-to-Kid View of How to Make Money, Make a Difference, and Have Fun Doing Both,* is the story of how he overcame bullying and his learning disability. Jack explores how he started his own business, and encourages other kids to do the same. He was a published author at the age of 12. He speaks to adults and children alike, spreading his story of courage and perseverance.

He is more confident, has bullyproof self-esteem, and knows at the core of his being that he can live the life of his dreams!

—Ann Morgan James
www.howtoraiseamillionaire.com

I hadn't thought about this in a long time, but in truth, it was one of the best experiences I ever had. When I was in grade 12, my friends and I loved making friendship bracelets out of plastic lace, which we called "gimp." We could make all kinds of different "weaves." Well, one day I saw some suede in a similar size to the gimp we used, and wondered what it would be like to make a bracelet with it. I tried it out, and the bracelet was really thick and uncomfortable. I was kind of bummed, because I was sure it was a great idea, and if I could come up with something people wanted, then I could make some extra money for myself (since my family didn't have a lot). So what next? I showed my grandmother, and she suggested that maybe I could make the bracelet into a key chain instead. I thought about it and played with the idea in my head for a while and then decided to give it a try. Behold! It worked, and it looked great. I showed it to some friends, and they loved it, too—so much, in fact, that they all wanted one. How much? How about three dollars? They asked what colors, and next thing I knew, I was taking orders for these key chains from friends, relatives, and *their* friends. Christmas was around the corner, so I was making about ten to fifteen of these key chains a night on top of my schoolwork, but I was loving it. I was so proud that people wanted something I made with my own hands, and I made some money to buy my family a couple of small things for Christmas that year.

—**Mary Lewis**
—**Luna Jewelz**
http://www.facebook.com/LunaJewelz

My story starts when I was about 6 years old, when I asked Santa for a record player for Christmas, and from that point on, I was always listening to music. Then, when I was 14, I ended up helping my brother as his assistant when he went out to DJ.

After a couple years of helping my brother, I had my first paid gig when I was 16 years old. It wasn't long after that when I started getting requests from folks who had attended events that I DJ'd. As the years rolled on it became something I enjoyed so much that I found myself incredibly busy. Twenty-nine years later, I have started my own DJ training company. Now I train DJs all over the world. I still do events, and to date I have entertained at over 1,300 events.

My son now goes out with me, and he is becoming quite the entrepreneur himself. Just like him, I don't view what I do as work.

I view it as my passion and a chance to pass on what I have learned over the past three decades of being in the DJ business.

Thanks for including me.

—**Mark Sferrazza**

DJTrainingAcademy.com

Conclusion

One thing in life I am certain of is that what you focus on expands. This book is a perfect example of this. If someone had told me a few years back that I would write a book one day, I would have thought that would be a good idea, *one day*. But a book about *money*? No way! It was going to be about horses—that was what I really knew about. Once the idea struck, and I knew that it was the right thing, I focused on what needed to happen to get this done. And that's it. Every day, I knew that it was going to happen, and made some small step in that direction. If there was something I didn't know how to do, I asked someone or I figured it out. I faced many fears: *Who am I to write this? I have never done this before. What if people don't like it? English was not one of my best subjects. I can't spell.* And on and on. The reason that none of those fears stopped me is that my focus was on what I needed to do to get one step closer to this goal. All I had to do was chunk it down into bite-size portions.

You can do the same thing. This book is not designed to read and complete in a week. It is something that I hope you will refer back to for months and years. When your children get to the stage of development where they are ready to venture forward, this book will still apply. It is designed to do ever so much more than teach your kids about money and business. It is about *believing* in your kids, investing time in your kids, and building the relationship you have (or perhaps don't have yet). It is about creating habits around spending, making, saving, and investing money that will help them never stress about the level of debt our society is designed to be in. It is about showing them a different concept from what they see on TV and in movies. It's about listening to their dreams and standing behind them as they reach to achieve them, and being ready to catch them and stand them back up when things don't go as planned. It's about standing at the finish line and cheering them on when they achieve those dreams, and about seeing their victories and challenges create a self-confident, independent, creative adult who will contribute to this world on many levels.

It is not your responsibility to decide if and when your child creates a business. They may be totally satisfied with their house chores and paycheck. They may do this for months or years before they go for something more. It's important they know you are ready to help and support them when they are ready. They may run in one day and say, "Mom, Dad, I have an idea!" And you will be ready to guide them to the next step.

It is your responsibility to teach your kids about how to manage their money and the importance of giving back in this world, whether with their money or with their time. Can you imagine if everyone in the world reached out their hand to help someone every day? I can. One family at a time, one child at a time. And two friends learn from her, and so on and so on and so on. Your child can change the world, just as mine are. They are never too little (or too old) to make a difference.

Take your time and enjoy this book. Read it over and over if you choose. Take the time to do all the exercises with your kids. It will create some fun and interesting conversations. Lead by example with the jar system. When you buy the new carpet or book that vacation, talk about how you did that.

Bring money into your everyday conversations—when you are at the grocery store, when the bills come in, at Christmastime. "Money" is not a secret word or subject to be whispered about. Those who think so are often those in financial trouble. Open up the conversation so that your kids feel comfortable asking questions. The more they know, the better prepared they will be in life.

Money is not everything. But having it can open up doors for you and your kids, can give both you and them more choices, and can help other people. Focus on the positive things that money makes possible, and be grateful for what you have now. This attitude will continue to bring money into your world and your kid's world.

I hope this book brought you some laughs, some ideas, some joy, and maybe even some tears.

What I loved most about this journey with my daughters was getting to see them grow in their skills, their thinking, the way they viewed the world in an ever-expanding capacity, the way they felt about themselves and what they could accomplish, the way that contributing to the world and making a difference became a part of their everyday thoughts. Not only did they grow as young ladies, but our time together growing, sharing, being creative, building rabbit hutches, teaching them how to use a cordless drill, seeing them bring in their first dollar, helping them mourn the death of a prize bunny, are memories that I will cherish for a lifetime. And I think they will, too.

Many people don't have the money to go out and spend a lot on entertainment and travel. But right there in their own homes they can build and create dreams that can take them to a better financial place as a family. It is time to stop looking to the world to solve our problems, and look within our families to create the life we desire.

So my wish to you and your family is that you experience the joy, growth, challenge, and excitement that I have with my kids— that you really get to discover who they are and what they are capable of, and that you give to the world a child who will make positive changes in it. I also wish for you to see your kids grow to create an abundant future in health, happiness, and finances.

Together we can change the world.

—**Gail Haynes**

About the Author

From an early age, Gail Haynes thought about how she could earn money to buy what she wanted. In the early days, those things were such vitally important stuff as candy and toys. Gail made crafts and sold them, held yard sales, and operated lemonade stands. At 16, she started Five Star Ranch, a western trail-riding facility. After graduating from high school and college, Gail expanded the farm and began to offer lessons and clinics and more. She even opened an on-site store catering to horse people. Today, twenty-six years later, Five Star Ranch is still going strong.

The common thread with all the money Gail made was that it disappeared almost the moment she earned it. Gail came from a family of spenders, so she learned that you earn a dollar, you spend a dollar. When she was growing up there was never any talk of saving or investing, and definitely not of giving to charity. So even though she was experiencing great success in her business, there was always an undertone (often a scream) of financial struggle. After finding herself more than a hundred thousand dollars deep in credit card debt, she even looked at bankruptcy.

When her daughters were 2 and 4 years old Gail became a single mom. Quickly the money ran out, the electricity was turned off, and she knew that something had to change. She didn't want her kids ever to experience the financial roller coaster that she was living on.

So Gail began teaching her kids about how to earn and manage their money. They grew curious about how to make more money, by having their own lemonade stands and making and selling handicrafts. When her kids were 7 and 9 they got pet rabbits; a boy and a girl (oops). Well, soon enough, they had baby rabbits, and a new business was born: Bunnyville, "where happiness comes a-hoppin.'" Seven years later, they have fifteen breeding rabbits, manage their own advertising, and have over a thousand fans on their Facebook fan page. They manage their business and personal money and understand the value of a dollar.

Gail has been a teacher and coach for twenty-four years. She has traveled Canada and the United States teaching seminars. Currently, she is running a Podcast to encourage Money Smart Kids, with fan pages to raise awareness on what kids can do. She's in the process of creating a membership site, has a blog page, and has a book called *The Lemonade-Stand Millionaire: A Parents' Guide to Encouraging the Entrepreneurial Spirit in Your Kids.*

Several newspapers and television programs have featured Gail as a successful young entrepreneur. She was acknowledged by the mayor of Oakville, who attended the grand opening of her indoor arena. She has mentored and encouraged many young people to start their own businesses, to see how they can create financial freedom doing something they love.

For much of the past sixteen years, Gail has travelled the world (Los Angeles, New York, British Columbia, the Virgin Islands, and more) to find the best educators in money management, marketing, and self-improvement. She has studied with masters such as Jay Abraham, Anthony Robbins, T. Harv Eker, John Grey, Courtney Smith, Keith Cunningham, Joel Roberts, Brendon Burchard, Rick Frishman, and many more. Gail passes on the lessons learned to her audience so they, too, can live a life of financial freedom.

In conclusion, Gail is dedicated to helping parents and kids learn how to create and manage money. The world is in financial crisis because of our borrow-and-spend mentality, so we need to reach kids now to stop the cycle of living from paycheck to paycheck, buried deep in debt.

Appendix A. Advantage of Early Investing

This information is intended to illustrate the value of investing early to take advantage of compounding investment returns, to generate superior growth.		Comparing the three scenarios The following is a summary of your three scenarios, showing total deposits, growth on these deposits, and accumulated value of your investments.	
Scenario 1		Scenario 1	
Start Age	10		
End Age	65	Total Deposits	$19,830
Initial Deposit Amount	$30	Growth	$693,351
Periodic Deposit Amount	$30	Accumulated Value	$713,181
Deposit Frequency	Monthly		
Annual Rate of Return	10.00%		
Scenario 2		Scenario 2	
Start Age	20		
End Age	65	Total Deposits	$16,230
Initial Deposit Amount	$30	Growth	$256,420
Periodic Deposit Amount	$30	Accumulated Value	$272,650
Deposit Frequency	Monthly		
Annual Rate of Return	10.00%		
Scenario 3		Scenario 3	
Start Age	40		
End Age	65	Total Deposits	$9,030
Initial Deposit Amount	$30	Growth	$28,295
Periodic Deposit Amount	$30	Accumulated Value	$37,325
Deposit Frequency	Monthly		
Annual Rate of Return	10.00%		
		There's a huge lesson here: starting at an early age will build a far greater accumulated value than starting later in life.	

The information contained here is for illustration purposes only. No warranty is made as to its accuracy.

Appendix B. Money Tracking Worksheets

PLAY				
Time for fun! Make a list of all the things that you can do to enjoy your money, such as toys, trips, outings, shows, sporting activities —You name it! Fill in the chart below, recording deposits $ (putting money in your jar) and withdrawals (when you spend it).				
Date	Deposit Type	Deposit Amount	Withdrawal Amount	Balance

Appendix B. Money Tracking Worksheets

LEARN				
This area is for anything that helps you learn. Put money in your jars for anything that will make you smarter, like a book, lessons, workshops, seminars, etc. Make sure you show your deposits and withdrawals and track your balance.				
Date	Deposit Type	Deposit Amount	Withdrawal Amount	Balance

Appendix B. Money Tracking Worksheets

PLAN				
Do you want a new bike or computer or have anything that you are saving for? Post it somewhere so you can see it every day. When you buy it, record in your withdrawal column and decide on next goal. (Jot in margin what current goal is)				
Date	Deposit Type	Deposit Amount	Withdrawal Amount	Balance

Appendix B. Money Tracking Worksheets

NECESSITIES				
This is your tracking sheet for when you start having living expenses or for 1 year before you move out on your own. This is also good for parents for groceries, mortgage, clothes, and other living expenses.				
Date	Deposit Type	Deposit Amount	Withdrawal Amount	Balance

Appendix B. Money Tracking Worksheets

WEALTH				
This area is for the money you are investing and growing for a secure and prosperous future. Add in interest from your investments when you earn it. Also, record the amount you transfer out of the jar to an investment. Your parents can help you here.				
Date	Deposit Type	Deposit Amount	Withdrawal Amount	Balance

Appendix B. Money Tracking Worksheets

ANGEL				
Here is your chance to make a difference. Deposit money in here to help charities, feed the hungry, help abused animals, etc. When you take money out to give to the special place or person, write it in the withdrawal column.				
Date	Deposit Type	Deposit Amount	Withdrawal Amount	Balance

Appendix C. Cash Jar Worksheets

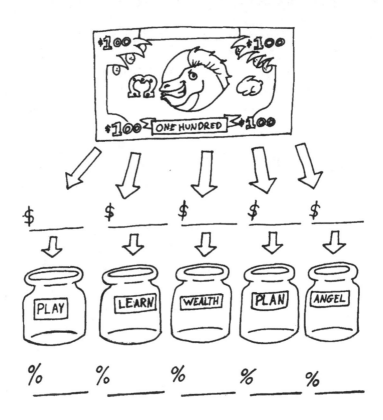

In the exercise above, take the $100 and practice dividing it up into its appropriate jar.

1. Choose the percentage for each category. (For suggestions, see chapter 4, "Teaching Kids How to Handle Money.")
2. Divide the $100 according to the chosen percentages.

Appendix C. Cash Jar Worksheets

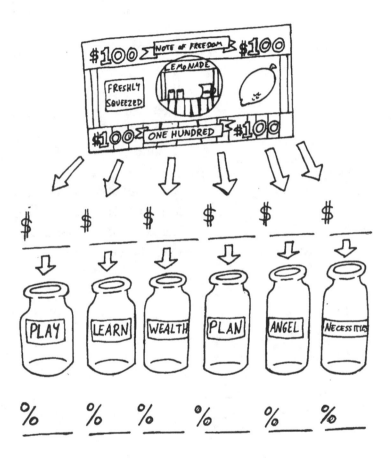

In the exercise above, take the $100 and practice dividing it up into its appropriate jar.

1. Choose the percentage for each category. (For suggestions, see chapter 4, "Teaching Kids How to Handle Money.")
2. Divide the $100 according to the chosen percentages.

Appendix D. What Goes Where

Have your kids help decide what category the following expenses go under.

N-Necessities   **P**-Play   **PL**-Plan   **W**-Wealth   **A**-Angel

Trip to the zoo	_____	IPod	_____
Milk and eggs	_____	Soccer Ball	_____
Toys	_____	Hockey Stick	_____
Computer	_____	Pet kitten	_____
Dictionary	_____		
Singing Lessons	_____		
Ice Cream	_____		
World Wildlife Fed.	_____		
Silver and Gold	_____		
Food Bank	_____		
Books	_____		
Stocks	_____		
Women's Shelter	_____		
Bicycle	_____		
Music CD	_____		
Fast Food	_____		
Night at the theater	_____		

Now add some of your own items. Choose both the things you *would like* to have and the things you need to have.

Some items could go in several categories. A computer, for example, could be either "education" or "plan." A hockey stick could be "fun," depending on how expensive it is. Remind your kids that they do not have to use "necessity" yet, but they will when they are older.

Appendix E. Household Chores Contract

This agreement is entered into on (Month/Day/Year) _____

between (Worker/Child) _____

and (Employer/Parent) _____

I agree to complete the following activities on a daily basis:

_____

_____

I agree to complete the following activities on a weekly basis:

_____

_____

I agree to complete the following activities on a monthly basis:

_____

_____

I agree that if I do not do 5 out of the 7 days of daily chores or 100% of weekly chores, I do not get paid for the week.

I agree that if I do not do my monthly chores, I will lose one week's pay.

I agree that I will do these on my own without constant reminders.

Signature _____ Date_____
                        (worker/child)

Signature _____ Date_____
                        (employer/parent)

Appendix F. Supplies Chart

Business Name: _____

Needed Supplies	Have it	Need it	Buy	Gifted	Borrowed	Returned

Total start up cost: _____

I agree to pay $ _____
for the _____
By (date) _____
Signature _____
Print Name _____

I agree to borrow the following supplies _____
To be returned by (date) _____
Signature _____
Print Name _____

Appendix G. Resources

The following is a list of sites that you and your kids can use to get business ideas, get products and services at very low cost, and promote and sell your business.

You will also find a link to attend a Millionaire Mind Seminar, at no charge, in a city near you.

The best part is, most of the sites are free to use. Don't forget the sites we talked about throughout the book. Take some time and look through them to see if they can be helpful to you.

Enjoy surfing the sites!

Millionairemindticket.com: For free tickets to an upcoming Millionaire Mind Intensive in a city near you, go to link and add in Ambassador # - MMI4570.

ClickBank.com: A great place to purchase or sell digital products such as e-books or audio or video products.

YouTube.com: The largest video sharing site on the Web. YouTube lets anyone upload short videos for private or public viewing. A great place to learn new skills, get inspired, or promote your own business. Set up a channel of your own.

Fiverr.com: Fiverr is a marketplace for "gigs" or jobs, that are priced at five dollars. You can sell and buy tasks for five dollars. So anyone can create a gig for small service on the site, and visitors can accept gigs as well. Categories include Social Marketing, Graphics,

Writing, Technology, Business, Silly Stuff, and Programming. I have personally used this site for a variety of gigs.

Online-stopwatch.com: A great site for timers for the exercises in the book or for other activities that you may want to time, such as homework time or chore time.

Ezine.com: Helps authors get exposure in exchange for submitting articles.

Audacity.sourceforge.net: Free software for recording and editing sounds. postproduction of all types of audio, including podcasts.

Mindmeister.com: Online mind-mapping software that enables users to visualize their thinking by creating maps of projects, business plans, event planning, and everyday life. A great organizational tool.

Mailchimp.com: Free e-mail marketing service. Design, send, and track e-mail campaigns with simple tools. Get a fully functional free account.

Want More?

Visit us at any of the following addresses to learn new information, be inspired by amazing kids' stories, and help your kids expand their knowledge and skills.

Blog Site: http://www.TheLemonadeStandMillionaire.com

Membership Site: http://www.MoneySmartKidsAcademy.com

(Get 3 free months with special offer at the end of the book)

Podcast: http://www.gailhaynes.podomatic.com/

Facebook:

http://www.facebook.com/MoneySmartKidsAcademy

http://www.facebook.com/TheLemonadeStandMillionaire

http://www.facebook.com/GailHaynesAuthor

Twitter: http://twitter.com/LSMillionaire

YouTube: http://www.youtube.com/user/KidsFinances

LinkedIn: http://www.linkedin.com then search Gail Haynes

Stay tuned for the follow-up workbooks for kids.

Claim Your Free Download — How to Raise Financially Independent Kids

As a special Bonus for purchasing this book you will receive a 5 part mini course. A series of tips to follow so you and your kids started today

Step 1. Go To lemonadestandmillionaire. com/get-your-free-download-here/

Step 2. Authenticate-(follow directions)

Step 3. Claim your free Gift sent to your inbox

Visit our Website!
TheLemonadeStandMillionaire.com

Visit our site today and meet other young entrepreneurs, read helpful articles, listen to informative podcasts and more, learn from experts in all areas of business and parenting and money.

Discover our members only area and get one month FREE ACCESS with the following code- LSMEM. Enjoy meeting others in our forum, get your questions answered, get exclusive video lessons, and more member's only bonuses.

Stay in touch, I want to hear your stories! Drop me a note on the contact page and your story could be featured on our site!

Gail Haynes

9 781614 483885